Jarrod Wilcox, CFA
Wilcox Investment Inc.

Jeffrey E. Horvitz
Moreland Management Company

Dan diBartolomeo
Northfield Information Services, Inc.

Investment Management for Taxable Private Investors

D1377544

RESEARCH FOUNDATION

OF CFA INSTITUTE

Statement of Purpose

The Research Foundation of CFA Institute is a not-for-profit organization established to promote the development and dissemination of relevant research for investment practitioners worldwide.

ISBN 0-943205-74-3

Printed in the United States of America

19 January 2006

Editorial Staff

Elizabeth A. Collins
Book Editor

David L. Hess
Assistant Editor

Kara H. Morris
Production Manager

Lois Carrier
Production Specialist

Biographies

Jarrod Wilcox, CFA, is president of Wilcox Investment Inc. He is the author of *Investing by the Numbers* and numerous articles in the *Journal of Portfolio Management, Financial Analysts Journal, Journal of Wealth Management,* and *Journal of Investing.* His investing experience includes work not only with private investors but also two decades with institutional investors in such roles as portfolio manager, director of research, and chief investment officer. Dr. Wilcox is a former faculty member of MIT's Sloan School of Management, where he also earned his PhD.

Jeffrey E. Horvitz is vice chairman of Moreland Management Company, a single-family investment office in operation for almost 20 years that actively invests in both public and private equity. He has published articles in such journals as the *Journal of Wealth Management* and the *Journal of Investing.* He has been a speaker at conferences for CFA Institute, the Boston Society of Security Analysts, the Institute for Private Investors, as well as at various financial industry conferences. Previously, Mr. Horvitz was an executive in a family real estate business. Mr. Horvitz holds MA degrees from both the University of Pennsylvania and the University of California at Los Angeles.

Dan diBartolomeo is president and founder of Northfield Information Services, Inc., which provides quantitative models of financial markets to nearly 300 investment institutions in 20 countries. He serves on the board of directors of the Chicago Quantitative Alliance and the executive body of the Boston Committee on Foreign Relations. Mr. diBartolomeo's writings include numerous papers in professional journals and the contribution of chapters in four different investment textbooks. He received his degree in applied physics from Cornell University.

Contents

Foreword

Investment management for taxable individuals is immensely complex. This complexity arises from the tax code, the naturally varied needs and wants of individuals and families, and the densely layered management and brokerage structure of the financial services industry. Yet, little rigorous research has been done on private wealth management. In fact, when David Montgomery and I wrote "Stocks, Bonds, and Bills after Taxes and Inflation," which appeared in the Winter 1995 *Journal of Portfolio Management*, we received a number of letters from financial planners and others concerned with private asset management, saying that, as far as the letter writers knew, we had addressed matters of concern to them for the first time. (It wasn't true, but that was their perception.) These managers toiling away on behalf of individual investors and their families are, of course, responsible for more assets than any other category of manager (most wealth is held by individuals, not pensions, foundations, or endowments), but, rightly or wrongly, they felt neglected and unguided in their pursuit of the goals common to all investors: higher returns, lower risk, and reasonable costs.

In *Investment Management for Taxable Private Investors*, a trio of distinguished authors—Jarrod Wilcox, Jeffrey E. Horvitz, and Dan diBartolomeo—do much to correct this imbalance. They begin by noting that private investors are much more diverse than institutional investors. This assertion is perhaps contrary to intuition. But viewed from the perspective of a private asset manager who is juggling the varied risk tolerances, cash flow needs, and balance sheet complexities of a family of private wealth holders, institutional investors do, indeed, all look pretty much the same. Taxation, at both the federal and state level in the United States, or in comparable jurisdictions in other countries, adds a thick layer of difficulty, which is exemplified by the fact that the U.S. Internal Revenue Code (just that one jurisdiction) is 9,000 pages long.

The authors begin with a strong review of finance theory, and to the usual litany of core concepts, they add stochastic growth theory, which has a grand history in the formal literature of finance but which has been little used. They note that because financial theory is an intentional oversimplification of reality, it is an even greater oversimplification when applied to private wealth management.

In the next section of the monograph, the authors review the principal asset classes and strategies that are used to benefit the private investor, with special attention paid to taxes and to maximizing after-tax returns. They also comment on the varied wealth levels, consumption patterns, and attitudes the private asset management practitioner is likely to encounter.

A particularly valuable section of the monograph deals with the organizational challenges faced by a private wealth management firm or practice. Providing customized investment services to a diverse population of choosy clients is difficult and costly. The authors describe a "portfolio manufacturing" approach that allows the firm to address this challenge profitably.

In the concluding section, the authors turn to the specialized problems of asset location, concentrated portfolios, and benchmarking. Asset location is the question of whether a given investment is (considering all factors, including other assets held by the investor) most tax efficient in a taxable or tax-deferred account. The asset location problem is made more complicated by the proliferation of types of tax-deferred accounts and by frequent tax law changes. In addition, portfolios that are concentrated in a single stock or industry are common among private investors and present a special challenge; liquidating the position all at once is not typically tax efficient, and some asset owners do not want it liquidated. Wilcox, Horvitz, and diBartolomeo describe several approaches to reducing the risk caused by such a concentrated position. Finally, the problems of establishing suitable benchmarks and of conducting progress evaluations for private wealth portfolios are addressed.

Just about all of us are private investors at some level. Thus the lessons in this monograph are valuable to all of us—not only to providers of private asset management services but also to consumers of them. For these reasons, the Research Foundation is extremely pleased to present *Investment Management for Taxable Private Investors*.

Laurence B. Siegel
Research Director
The Research Foundation of CFA Institute

Preface

The amount of published research in finance is large, but the amount of work devoted to issues that are important to private investors is a small percentage of the total, and the amount that is available pales in comparison to the needs of investors. Nevertheless, we wish to acknowledge the pioneering work of a handful of people who made overall contributions to the concepts and practice of managing investments for private investors. Their work was an inspiration for our investigations.

Early academic theoretical work by George Constantinides demonstrated that decisions about recognizing capital gains could be treated as option valuation problems. Another early influence on work in this field was William Fouse, who argued compellingly at the end of the 1960s that index funds were more tax efficient than the actively managed funds of the day. More recently, William Reichenstein, John Shoven, and several others began the study of tax-deferred savings accounts. David Stein, Robert Arnott, and Jean Brunel have written extensively on improving after-tax returns—in particular, on how active management can be modified for private (taxable) investors. In a sense, their intellectual godfather was Robert Jeffrey (1993), a demanding private wealth client who stimulated management firms focusing on institutional investors to come up with something better than what was then available for taxable investors.[1]

Despite the efforts of such authors, we believe that the taxable investor could be much better served by the investment community than it has been, and we commend the Research Foundation of CFA Institute for its efforts to redress this imbalance. This book was motivated by the taxable investor's needs:

- Private investors are much more diverse than institutional investors. The differences are related primarily to their amount of wealth, their needs, and their desires (which usually change over time) for consumption and to leave a legacy, their tax posture (which can vary from year to year), and how they personally value changes in wealth.

- Finance theory involves much simplification of real-world problems, and this simplification is even more pronounced when theory is applied to private investors.

- For individual investors, taxation is one of the most important aspects of investment performance, policy, and strategy—as important as pretax risk and return. The U.S. tax code is complex, however, and contains both traps and opportunities. How it applies and how it affects each private investor can be highly specific to circumstances that may change significantly over time.

---

[1]The list of references in this book contains many more works that provide details on various specific topics.

- Investment professionals cannot adequately serve the private investor without customizing services toward a "market of one." Whether this customization is highly personal or nearly automated, it cannot be a "one size fits all" approach. The standardized rules and methods that can work well for the institutional investor are likely to fail the private investor.

Organization and Topics

We began with some ideas we wanted to get across with respect to obtaining better after-tax returns. As the book progressed, however, we realized that the needs of the professional investment manager who is used to serving institutional clients were much broader than we had previously thought. For example, how does one deal with investors who, unlike institutional investors, have limited life spans and, consequently, a somewhat predictable pattern of changing needs? How does the professional investment management organization cope with the order-of-magnitude increases in customization and complexity required for truly responsive private wealth management? Specifically, what does one do to cope with such tricky problems as a large concentrated position in low-cost-basis stock? What does the world look like from the wealthy investor's viewpoint, and what changes in attitude are required of the professional manager with an institutional background? To address this wide range of topics, we divided the book into four parts:

I A Conceptual Framework for Helping Private Investors,

II Private Wealth and Taxation,

III Organizing Management for Private Clients, and

IV Special Topics (location, concentrated risk, and benchmarking).

Although each chapter of the book was written by a designated author or authors, we read, edited, and discussed one another's work extensively. The chapter responsibilities were as follows:

- Jarrod Wilcox, CFA: Chapters 1, 2, and 3, and Appendices A and B;
- Jeffrey Horvitz: Chapters 4, 5, 6, and 11; and
- Dan diBartolomeo: Chapters 7 and 8.

Chapter 9 was jointly authored by Dan diBartolomeo and Jeffrey Horvitz, and all three authors wrote Chapter 10. We hope the reader enjoys reading the book as much as we enjoyed collaborating in the synthesis of its ideas.

The reader will discover in this book useful information, presented with a minimum of mathematics, on the following topics:[2]

- challenges in investing private wealth;
- proper application of academic theory to practical private wealth management;
- life-cycle planning for various stages of wealth, life expectancy, and desires for wealth transfer;
- differing needs by wealth level;
- the U.S. federal taxation of investments;
- obtaining a tax alpha—or achieving the best practical after-tax returns;
- adapting institutional money management for serving high-net-worth investors;
- private portfolio management as a manufacturing process;
- individual retirement plans and the issue of which securities to locate in them;
- combining risk management with tax concerns in dealing with concentrated risk positions.

In several chapters, the reader will see data such as maximum applicable rates and other statutory numbers in the tax code in braces, { }. We have used data that were applicable *at the time this book was written*, and the braces are to remind the reader that tax rates and tax code metrics may become out of date because they are subject to legislative change. The reader is cautioned not to assume that the numbers in braces will be in effect in the future.

Acknowledgments

We wish to express our appreciation to the Research Foundation of CFA Institute for encouraging us to prepare this treatment of topics of special interest to investment professionals serving private clients. We also wish to give special thanks to Robert Gordon, Steven Gaudette, and David Boccuzzi, who were kind enough to read the draft and suggest changes, and to Milissa Putman for excellence in document preparation.

Dan diBartolomeo
Jeffrey E. Horvitz
Jarrod Wilcox, CFA
Massachusetts
August 2005

---

[2] Annuities and life insurance are central to the financial planning of many private investors not at the upper end of the wealth spectrum. In this book, however, we concentrate on those investment needs of individual investors that are not addressed through annuities or other insurance products.

Part I
A Conceptual Framework for
Helping Private Investors

Chapter 1 points to some of the perhaps difficult attitudinal changes needed for an investment advisor or management organization to successfully work with wealthy private clients—including a willingness to accept customization and deal with complexity and a more proactive view of fiduciary responsibility than is needed when working with institutional clients. Chapter 2 draws from and adapts useful academic theories to the task of managing private money while cautioning against the many mistakes that may be made if theory is not applied with sufficient consideration of the real complexities involved. Chapter 3 applies these concepts to construct a consistent approach to lifetime investing that is flexible enough to deal properly with the differences in age and financial outcomes advisors meet in private investors.

1. Introduction and Challenge

The client, a U.S. businessman, was astonished to see that his investment advisory firm had mistakenly rebalanced his family's stock portfolio in the same way as for portfolios of its tax-exempt pension fund accounts. The resulting enormous tax bill was this investor's introduction to the culture gap that can sometimes exist between professionals serving institutional and private investors. An even wider gulf separates most academic research from the empirical world of private investors. Pragmatic professional investors often find the teachings of theoretical finance inapplicable.

Academics, professional institutional investors, and private investors—all have insights that can contribute to effective management of private wealth. Our purpose in this book is to provide an integrated view aimed at enhancing the value of the services professional investment managers and advisors provide to private investors.

Challenges in Investing Private Wealth

Private investors differ widely in their needs not only from tax-exempt institutions but also from one another—and even from themselves at different points in their lives. Consequently, effective private wealth investing requires a high degree of *customization*. Largely because of taxation, investing private wealth is also *complex*. And private investors usually need help from those willing to take *fiduciary responsibility*. Each of these factors poses significant challenges for the professional investment manager.

Need for Customization. Private investors differ from tax-exempt investors, and from each other, in many ways that affect best investment practice. Under a progressive income tax regime like that in the United States, different investors have different marginal income tax rates. They also live in different states, paying different state tax rates. Capital gains taxes differ from taxes on ordinary income; capital gains taxes are levied on the profit, but usually only upon liquidation of the security position.

One private investor may have a life expectancy of 10 years; another, of 30 years. Goals for possible wealth transfer before or at the end of life also differ widely. Some want to pass wealth on to their children; others want to support a charitable cause. Some just want to make sure that they do not outlive their wealth. For some investors, the issue of a proper balance between current income and capital appreciation may be a delicate intergenerational family matter; for others, it may be a matter of indifference—except for tax considerations. Private investors have different sizes of portfolios, so an investment management structure that is too costly for one is inexpensive for another.

Private investors differ in their risk attitudes and in their desires for active management. They may have extensive business interests or low-cost-basis stocks that need special diversification. Some investors want to be very involved in the details of their wealth management in order to keep a feeling of control of their personal capital; some are content to delegate. Private investors may be in the wealth accumulation and savings mode or in the wealth preservation and spending mode.

The needs of tax-exempt entities are much more homogeneous and more amenable to standardized approaches than the needs of private investors. The first challenge for institutional investment managers, then, is to focus on the investor's individual needs. Doing this properly requires special knowledge and an approach and cost structure that allow considerable customization—not only for the extraordinarily wealthy but also for the much larger group of investors who need and are willing to pay for professional services.

Inherent Complexity. Even after adequate customization has been defined, the investment professional's job remains much more complex than would be a similar role serving a pension fund. Private investors, perhaps mostly for tax reasons, often have a complex system of "buckets" in which wealth of different types and tax efficiency is located. These buckets may be as basic as a bank account and a retirement plan or as complicated as a wealthy family's business, a taxable personal portfolio, multiple trusts for the owners and their children, various limited partnerships, and a private foundation. Different investment policies may be appropriate for different buckets, depending on tax rules, family members' needs, and the planned end-of-life disposition of wealth. The investor needs coordinated investment policies and procedures among the buckets.

For each bucket, the system of tax rules may be complex and highly nonlinear, even for an investor of moderate wealth. Depending on nation (or even state) of domicile, an investor holding a simple common stock portfolio may face different taxes on dividends, short-term capital gains, and long-term capital gains. Complex rules govern the extent to which net losses can be carried forward into future years, the potential for tax-loss harvesting, and the need to avoid "wash sale" penalties. Finally, wealth transfer taxes, such as estate and gift taxes, have their own complicated requirements that can influence what the optimal decisions are in earlier years.

This complexity implies that practices learned elsewhere for gaining extra return while managing risk may give investment managers the wrong answer. For example, attempting to add to expected pretax return by active management may, instead, reduce after-tax return. The application of mean–variance optimization as usually practiced may give a poor answer to the question of what to do with a concentrated position of low-cost-basis stock or how to best take advantage of opportunities for deferring taxes through loss realization.

The challenge for professional managers is to take this complexity seriously, to quantify the value to be added by giving it due attention, and to balance that value against the benefits from devoting resources to other activities—for example, forecasting security returns or communicating with clients.

Fiduciary Responsibility. An institutional investment manager may be involved mostly in some combination of the quest for returns superior to a benchmark and the quest to control tracking error around a benchmark. Adequate fiduciary responsibility for this manager is relatively easy: The scope of the assignment and the complexity of the client's needs are limited, and the investment sophistication of the client is relatively high—not so in working with private clients. In many such cases, the investment advisor's responsibility extends to advice on how much risk to take and on generating after-tax returns, help in selecting not only securities but also other investment managers, and long-term financial planning. The stakes, at least for the client, are high. And the amount of accurate investment knowledge clients have may be very low.

Some private clients lack information about investments, are distrustful of financial matters, and may be too conservative for their own good. Others, particularly those who have created wealth in a conventional business career, mistakenly believe their personal experience to be transferable to the arena of the liquid securities markets and are overconfident. These attitudes are often reinforced by the popular media, with their emphasis on financial heroes who have experienced unusually good results, and even by professional investment research, which is generally optimistically biased and gives too much importance to recent developments. The popular investment press is filled with "do-it-yourself" articles implying that investing is both simple and obvious. But most clients need help of a type that they do not know enough about to request. In general, to fulfill their fiduciary responsibility, investment professionals must be proactive with private clients.

The importance of this challenge deserves what might at first seem to be a digression on ethics—that is, achieving good business through good practice.

Good Practice in Working with Private Clients

In serving private clients, especially if one comes from the world of competitive investment performance, the ethical standards that stand out relate to (1) the costs of customizing versus its value and (2) the possible short-term loss of revenues through educating clients about realistic long-term expectations.

CFA Institute maintains that ethical standards are good business. Consider these excerpts from the list of standards to which holders of the Chartered Financial Analyst designation are expected to adhere, together with our queries:[1]

> When Members and Candidates are in an advisory relationship with a client, they must:
>
> a. Make a reasonable inquiry into a client's or prospective client's investment experience, risk and return objectives, and financial constraints prior to making any investment recommendation or taking investment action and must reassess and update this information regularly.
> b. Determine that an investment is suitable to the client's financial situation and consistent with the client's written objectives, mandates, and constraints before making an investment recommendation or taking investment action.
> c. Judge the suitability of investments in the context of the client's total portfolio.

Query: Does not this standard mean that after-tax returns and their associated risks should be the focus for private investors rather than pretax returns and risks? How important is tracking error relative to absolute risk?

> **Performance Presentation.** When communicating investment performance information, Members or Candidates must make reasonable efforts to ensure that it is fair, accurate, and complete.
>
> **Misrepresentation.** Members and Candidates must not knowingly make any misrepresentations relating to investment analysis, recommendations, actions, or other professional activities.

Query: Is it enough to say that "past performance is not a guarantee of future success," or should investment managers educate clients with regard to the modest extent to which performance history is evidence of future success? Should discussion of product features that are attractive in the short run be balanced by explanations of the less favorable implications for longer-term and after-tax outcomes?

Meeting such requirements set forth by the CFA Institute Standards of Professional Conduct is particularly challenging when true suitability requires costly customization and record keeping for the most-effective tax management and when most private clients require education if they are to avoid damaging decisions. Private clients need education to avoid misunderstanding the significance of performance data, and they need it to help them understand the long-term implications of such appealing product features as high current income or downside protection.

Private clients with smaller portfolios have not been able to obtain some of the customized treatment we advocate, although this situation is beginning to change with the advent of greater computer automation. They have also been hard to convince to pay directly for advice because so much of the support for their financial planning comes through sales commissions. The result has been conflicts of interest that make client education and full fiduciary responsibility problematic. Said

---

[1] Standards are from the CFA Institute Standards of Professional Conduct (www.cfainstitute.org).

another way, private investors are more expensive than institutional clients for a financial services company to serve well. Either the fees for excellent professional services will be high, possibly prohibitively so for investors of moderate wealth (as they are today), or the investment professional must adopt methods that are both likely to bring about good investment outcomes and are cost-effective to implement. As improved tools bring down the cost of lifetime financial planning, risk management, and tax management, however, and as managers learn to communicate the value of these processes, the opportunity for profitable fiduciary responsibility seems likely to increase.

Case Example

The case mentioned in the chapter's opening was real. In the early 1980s, a large family fund was invested with a high-flying quantitative boutique manager given the assignment of maintaining a rather passive but highly quantitatively managed stock portfolio. The combination of a charismatic chief executive, leading-edge technologies, and a terrific track record had attracted many new accounts to this boutique. One of them was just a little different. In contrast to other accounts handled by the firm, this account was tax sensitive. The firm, however, was more investment centered than client centered in the management of the portfolios in its care. The portfolio manager had developed a number of computerizations of formerly manual processes. He favored passive portfolios with a computerized procedure for rebalancing the portfolios back toward their benchmarks. On the fateful day of the first rebalancing of the family fund, the identifier of the account was not excluded from a computer file to be read by a computerized trading program. The consequence was a massive and unnecessary tax bill.

Summary

The professional investor who is used to managing institutional portfolios faces special challenges when serving private investors:
- the need for customization because of differences in investor situations,
- a huge increase in complexity caused by taxation rules and interlinked portfolios, and
- broader fiduciary responsibilities for private clients, who may be poorly informed and who may need more all-inclusive help than institutional clients.

Good practice in working with private clients requires an ethical standard that
- goes beyond choosing suitable securities to encompass specific attention to after-tax returns and absolute versus relative risk and
- proactively avoids misrepresentation by including investor education in the job—for example, by pointing out how difficult it is to project past performance rather than by merely providing an accurate performance record.

These requirements make private investors more expensive to service than institutional clients and encourage the development of cost-effective ways to meet private clients' needs.

2. Theory and Practice in Private Investing

Private investors face far more complex decisions than do untaxed, long-lived institutions. Classical financial models, with their heroically simplified assumptions, cannot hope to present a complete picture of what private investors face, and using the models can even lead to worse results than using old-fashioned, less-theory-driven investment methods. This chapter addresses six key concepts of current finance theory as applied pragmatically to private investors:

1. the quasi-efficient market,
2. utility theory as applied to risk,
3. Markowitz portfolio optimization,
4. the capital asset pricing model (CAPM),
5. option valuation models, and
6. stochastic growth theory.

The Quasi-Efficient Market

Empirical academic research has amply confirmed that the liquid public securities markets are mostly efficient, in that the prices of securities incorporate publicly available information, so that it is difficult to make abnormal profits. We do not have to accept idealized theories of *perfect* instantaneous incorporation of new information to accept the stubborn empirical fact that security returns are hard to forecast. It is the "nearly" qualifier on return independence that gives employment to investment analysts and talented strategists and traders. But investors are well advised to base their strategies around a default position that presumes they will not be able to forecast most price fluctuations.

We *can* say that over long periods of time, stocks are likely to outperform bonds, but we cannot say with much confidence whether the stock market will go up tomorrow or which stock will have the best returns. It is hard to admit, but at any moment, much of what we know and much of what we have just learned is already incorporated in prices, at least for the heavily traded public markets. For the private investor who wishes to both outperform the market and delegate investing to someone else, the forecasting task has two layers. The investor must first choose a superior manager; then, the manager must choose the right security at the right time. The initial layer of the problem, selecting an above-average manager, is nearly of the same uncertainty and difficulty as the second layer of the problem—above-average security selection and timing. Competition among investment managers to exploit modest pockets of market inefficiency with which to earn above-average returns without excessive risk (the second layer), and thereby attract clients (the first layer), is intense.

Not only is the market for skillful managers itself competitive, with the more successful managers likely to attract so many clients that the initial extra-profitable investing niche is outgrown, but it is made murkier for the private investor by the confusion between good pretax and good after-tax return performance. To those who believe there is at least a modest statistical possibility of successfully investing with investment managers who exhibit a streak of high performance, we suggest that they consider the drag on after-tax performance from the increased effective tax rates triggered by turnover. While not wanting to discourage the pursuit of above-average returns through better forecasts within areas of market inefficiency, we believe that adding value to private client portfolios is far easier through reducing effective tax rates and through after-tax control of risk appropriate to the client's lifestyle needs and aspirations than it is through beating the market.

Utility Theory and Investment Risk Taking

More than a century ago, economic theories became popular that were based in the law of diminishing marginal utility with increasing wealth known with certainty. The reach of this concept was greatly extended after World War II, when it began to be used as a way to describe the fact that money received with certainty was preferable to a risky process with the same expected value. Utility curves mapped utility as a function of wealth. The utility of wealth known with certainty was presumed to lie on the curve, whereas the utility of mean expected values of an uncertain outcome between two possibilities was supposed to lie on a lower straight line connecting the two points. Different degrees of curvature represented different degrees of risk aversion. A utility function of declining risk aversion with increasing wealth could be represented by curves that got flatter as wealth increased.

Although utility curves can be used to construct illuminating theories, their use in practical application for private investors is problematic. Individuals have difficulty expressing the shape of their utility curves, and their responses can vary depending on the framing of questions and the time period involved. Even in simple cases, they usually cannot convert their utility curves for terminal wealth after many periods into the utility curve they would need for the single current period.

Therefore, advisors need a method for specifying connections between appropriate utility functions for the short run to produce optimal utility in the long run. The mean–variance optimization approach is an important building block in this direction but one that does not need to explicitly reference utility to be useful in practice.

Markowitz Mean–Variance Portfolio Optimization

Markowitz (1959) devised an approach for thinking about diversification based on maximizing a risk-adjusted expected portfolio return. More concretely, the expected portfolio return is expressed as the sum of individual security expected returns weighted by their proportions in the portfolio. The portfolio return variance is the sum of the elements of a weighted return covariance matrix. Each element in the matrix represents the risk contribution of a pair of securities. This contribution is the product of the proportions of each security in the portfolio, their standard deviations of return, and the correlation coefficient of their returns. Maximizing the risk-adjusted expected return constructed in this manner is known as portfolio mean–variance optimization.

The *efficient frontier* is the set of portfolios for which at a given risk, no higher expected return is to be had. The maximization of the Markowitz mean–variance objective consists of selecting that point on the efficient frontier that corresponds to the best outcome given the investor's trade-off between expected return and variance (or risk aversion). For a fairly wide variety of plausible utility curves, maximizing a linear function of mean expected return and variance can approximate maximizing utility, as long as the possible outcomes are not too extremely separated. This capability is simply the consequence of being able to fit a quadratic curve closely to any smooth curve within a local region.

For the private investor, taking taxes into account is especially important when providing inputs to the model. Examples are given in Appendix A and Appendix B.

Correctly specified, kept up to date, and restricted to the kinds of problems for which it is suited, period-by-period mean–variance optimization produces excellent long-term results. To avoid misusing it, the investment manager or advisor should be familiar with several potential pitfalls:

- misspecifying the input variables,
- focusing on the wrong kind of variance,
- not controlling for errors in inputs,
- overly narrow scope,
- inadequacy of return variance as a risk measure,
- need to update risk-aversion parameters, and
- significant links between periods.

If not handled with care, each of these issues can be more of a problem for private taxable investors than for institutional, tax-exempt investors. Brunel (2002) offered a view of the difficulties similar to this list but was less optimistic with regard to the potential for overcoming them.

Misspecifying the Input Variables. Taxable investors should use *after-tax* returns and risks as inputs to a Markowitz mean–variance analysis. An individual's tax-advantaged accounts, such as pension plans, should be treated as separate asset classes. For example, bonds held in an individual retirement account (and, consequently, having a low effective tax rate because of tax deferral) should be treated as a different asset class from bonds held in a taxable account. Returns from stocks {taxed at a 15 percent rate} are more tax advantaged than returns from taxable bonds {taxed at a 35 percent rate}; consequently, using pretax returns distorts the optimization for taxable investors.

Similar tax effects apply to estimates of risk. Taxation affects risk management because the government often acts as a risk-sharing partner. Here is a simplified example. Suppose an investment has an equal risk of a 15 percent gain or a 5 percent loss, and suppose the capital gains tax rate is 20 percent. Pretax, the mean gain will be 5 percent and the forecasted standard deviation will be 10 percent. After tax, the mean gain will be 4 percent and the standard deviation will be 8 percent (both have been reduced by 1/5). But rather than standard deviation, what is used in the optimizing calculation is the *variance* (standard deviation squared). The after-tax mean is 4/5 of the pretax mean, but the after-tax variance is only 16/25 of the pretax risk. Counterintuitively, the attractiveness of the risky asset relative to a risk-free asset is *increased* by taxation. As the applicable tax rate increases, generally, one should, all other things being equal, have a greater preference for assets with greater pretax risk. Of course, the qualification is that the taxable investor have enough unrealized gains elsewhere in the portfolio, or in the near future, to effectively use tax losses.

Focusing on the Wrong Kind of Variance. Institutional portfolio management often proceeds in stages, with long-term asset allocation leading to portions of the portfolio being farmed out to specialized investment managers within each asset class. To measure skill and to prevent the manager from deviating from the assigned mandate, the institution may place considerable emphasis on risk relative to a benchmark. This risk is typically measured as the squared standard deviation of differences in return from the benchmark, and it is inserted into mean–variance optimization in place of the absolute return variance. Such relative risk is of far less interest to private investors, however, who must be concerned with their portfolio as a whole. Because a focus on tracking error penalizes investment managers who reduce total portfolio risk, too much concern with relative risk and too little emphasis on absolute risk is a particular trap in professional management of private wealth.

Easily overlooked is the possibility of future tax changes, both through changes in tax law and through the investor's individual tax posture. Ideally, this "risk" should be incorporated in estimating after-tax risk and return; in other words, the potential for future changes in tax treatment is itself a source of after-tax return variance.

Not Controlling for Errors in Inputs. After a few years of attempting practical application, investment practitioners recognized that when mean–variance optimization is applied to large numbers of assets, the optimization problem as originally posed is unduly sensitive to errors in the input assumptions. And estimating effective tax rates aggravates the problem of uncertain inputs.

Fortunately, methods have been devised for managing at least the part of the problem that grows rapidly as the number of assets analyzed for the portfolio grows. These methods include (1) simplifying the covariance matrix by decomposing it into a smaller number of statistical common factors, (2) shrinking estimates toward prior beliefs not evident in the particular sample or model from which the original estimates were drawn (Ledoit 1999), and (3) trying out multiple assumptions and averaging the resulting optimal output proportions (Michaud 2001). Such methods are not necessary for an allocation among a few broad asset classes, but they are vital when dealing with numerous securities, as in the application of mean–variance optimization to day-to-day portfolio management.

Overly Narrow Scope. Institutional investors using Markowitz optimization usually do so for both conventional and alternative assets classes but almost always limit use to those classes with easily quantifiable market values. Private investors, however, are concerned with their total financial picture, which extends beyond liquid financial assets. Implied assets that may need to be taken into account include the value of a house or houses, perhaps a private family business, discounted stock options, unvested stock or stock options, and the capitalized saving stream from employment. Implied liabilities may include a home mortgage and the present value of any net spending (e.g., spending in excess of employment income), such as in retirement. To exclude these implied assets and liabilities is to assume that they do not vary in a way that would affect ideal holdings in marketable securities. Whether the extra effort required to include implied assets and liabilities is worthwhile will depend on the individual case.

Inadequacy of Variance as a Risk Measure. Markowitz recognized that investors object only to downside risk, not to upside risk. Usually, the relative downside risks of diversified portfolios are adequately ranked by their relative variances or, equivalently, by the square root of variance (standard deviation). However, return variance may not adequately capture the adverse impact of a rare but catastrophic outcome. Therefore, additional risk measures may be useful in some cases. For example, U.S. tax law has an asymmetrical requirement that high-tax-rate net *short-term losses* (net of short-term gains) be matched against low-tax-rate net *long-term gains* (net of long-term losses). This requirement, together with the requirement that further excess losses (short-term or long-term) be carried forward, introduces a substantial negative skew to the potential after-tax return distribution. This additional downside risk may be worth taking into account for a high-risk investment occupying a large proportion of a taxable portfolio.

Need to Update Risk-Aversion Parameters. Markowitz mean–variance optimization is often used as an aid in financial planning or asset allocation over long time horizons—five years being fairly typical. In the interim period, the professional advice is usually to rebalance back toward that strategic allocation when returns of asset classes move asset weights too far away from desired proportions. Of course, that advice should be tempered by tax considerations.

An important aspect is that, unless the full asset allocation analysis is redone more frequently than every five years, rebalancing does not deal with the fact that appropriate risk aversion may change as a function of substantial changes in wealth. This issue is particularly acute for private investors who experience major personal losses. Institutional investors, which are usually more professionally diversified, probably do not often get into a position where they are forced by losses to become more conservative to avoid disastrous shortfalls.

Significant Links between Periods. Transaction costs, although they imply an impact beyond the period in which they are incurred, are generally small enough that one can simply amortize the cost over the estimated prospective holding period. The savings in effective capital gains tax rates from compounding unrealized gains through long-term holdings (tax deferral) can be treated the same way. At times, however, planning that is more explicitly *multiperiod* is advisable. For example, a large tax payment may reduce discretionary wealth so much that potential changes in risk-aversion trade-offs need to be taken into account. An example is given in Appendix B.

The Capital Asset Pricing Model

The CAPM attempts to describe a security market in equilibrium. It assumes that each investor is a Markowitz mean–variance optimizer and that all investors process the same information in the same way; they differ only in their aversion to risk, expressed as return variance. Another key assumption is that each investor can lend or borrow at the same risk-free interest rate. The model also assumes either no taxes or that all investors are subject to the same tax rates. The CAPM implies that, among other things, a passive index fund holding the entire market of risky securities in proportion to their respective market values will be more efficient than any other portfolio.

The CAPM's assumptions are clearly unrealistic. For example, the same capitalization-weighted portfolio of risky assets cannot be optimal for both taxable and nontaxable investors. The practical issue, however, is not the realism of the assumptions but whether the model's predictions can be put to good use. Although extensive empirical research does not support several of the CAPM's predictions, it has found that market index funds, although not perfectly optimal, are good choices for taxable investors. The broad diversification of index portfolios, the low fees, and the low turnover (which allows capital gains taxes to be deferred for long periods) are a combination that has many desirable properties for the private investor.

Option Valuation Theory

Option securities convey the right, but not the obligation, to buy or sell a given underlying security at a given price and at (European option) or until (American option) a given time. The original Black–Scholes option valuation model is based on the insight that a stock option payoff can be replicated with a continuously changing basket of long and short positions involving only cash, bonds, and the underlying stock. The assumptions behind the model were not completely realistic, but the model's accuracy has been sufficient to produce a profound change in the way we understand option valuation: Option values depend on return variance in the underlying stock and are not generally a material function of expected return for the stock.

All private investors subject to capital gains taxes can benefit from a basic understanding of option valuation because the right but not the obligation to sell at a loss creates a tax benefit. The investor has an option to sell or not to sell, and so to realize a gain or loss throughout the holding period of the security. For any given tax lot, this option has a value that depends on the variance of the underlying security. Across a portfolio of various tax lots for the same security, the value of a portfolio of such options is enhanced by dispersion in the ratios of cost to price. The combined value of these individual security option portfolios is enhanced to the degree that the underlying risks are imperfectly correlated across stocks, so the option value can be obtained without the corresponding increase in portfolio variance that would result from systematic market risk.

Because of the option to realize a capital gain or loss, a taxable investor is (1) less hurt by portfolio risk than are tax-exempt investors, (2) better off owning multiple tax lots of the same stock bought at different prices, and (3) able to derive benefit from stock-specific risk (volatility). The result is a lower effective tax rate and higher expected after-tax returns.

Investment professionals who have spent their careers working with tax-exempt portfolios—where specific risks of individual stocks are something to be avoided— may be surprised at the idea of encouraging specific risk. The idea of cultivating dispersion in tax-lot ratios of price to cost may be even more foreign. Yet, the benefits to private investors in reducing effective tax rates through tax-loss harvesting can be material. This benefit supports the use of portfolios that are large in terms of more variety in security names, more tax lots, and more emphasis on a diversified list of relatively less correlated returns. In practice, these criteria can be met by a portfolio of many diversified small-capitalization stocks bought at different times to obtain cost variety.

Stochastic Growth Theory

In addition to the core concepts of finance discussed up to this point, we have long advocated stochastic growth theory as a useful approach to setting the risk-aversion parameter in mean–variance optimization for short time periods in such a way that they produce better long-term results (Wilcox 2003). The insights of this theory tell us that when one maximizes expected log return on *discretionary* wealth each period, the result tends to maximize median long-term total wealth. Rubinstein (1976) proposed a similar approach for incorporating investor preferences into market pricing theory.

Log return is calculated each period as the natural logarithm of the quantity 1 plus the conventional arithmetic return. To calculate compound return over multiple periods, subtract 1 from the antilog of the sum of the individual log returns. It can be shown that maximizing the expected log return in individual periods tends to maximize the median compound result in the long run.

The idea of maximizing expected log return on the total portfolio for individual periods to get the best compounding result has a long history, beginning with Bernoulli in the 1700s. Applied to the total portfolio in unmodified form, the approach does not account for the needs of conservative investors, but applying it to only the portion of the portfolio that is discretionary (i.e., that the investor can afford to lose) is a different matter. This limited approach will maximize the median growth of the discretionary wealth away from the shortfall point. It also imposes an extreme penalty if the portfolio's value comes near the shortfall point. By setting the shortfall point high enough, any degree of additional conservatism can be produced.

A Taylor series is a mathematical device for expressing a nonlinear function of some quantity as the sum of an infinite series of terms of increasing powers of the quantity. When expected log return is expressed as a Taylor series of the difference between outcomes and the expected arithmetic return, the result provides great insight into the impact of statistical characteristics of conventional arithmetic returns, such as mean, variance, skewness, and kurtosis. Each successive term provides incremental information about events of smaller probability but greater influence on compounding returns if they should occur.

For investors of limited human lifetimes, four terms are sufficient to consider in making current investment decisions. The advisor thereby takes into account not only the variance used in Markowitz mean–variance optimization but also excess downside risk represented by negative skew and so-called fat-tailed (high-kurtosis) return distributions.

In most practical cases involving diversified investment portfolios, the effects of even these third (skewness) and fourth (kurtosis) return moments are tiny and can be ignored. Then the objective of maximizing expected log return on discretionary wealth can be approximated using a formula derived from simplifying (for small to moderate expected arithmetic returns) only the first two terms of its Taylor series representation (Wilcox):

$$\text{Expected log return} \cong LE\left(1-T*\right)-\frac{L^2V\left(1-T*\right)^2}{2}, \tag{2.1}$$

where

L = ratio of total assets to discretionary wealth
E = pretax mean return
$T*$ = effective tax rate
V = pretax return variance

Maximizing this function provides an approach to analyzing financing decisions. But in the more typical case where no changes in the ratio of total assets to discretionary wealth are permitted, this objective can also be achieved approximately by dividing it by the resulting constant leverage, L, and maximizing

$$E\left(1-T*\right)-\frac{LV\left(1-T*\right)^2}{2}. \tag{2.2}$$

This objective is simply *Markowitz mean–variance optimization with after-tax means and variances and with the trade-off for risk aversion set to L/2*, or half the ratio of assets to discretionary wealth. In other words, rather than asking the investor to identify a subjective aversion to near-term risk, the advisor, assuming a goal of maximizing long-term median outcomes, objectively determines an optimum aversion to this risk based on the investor's specification of a shortfall point.

Figure 2.1 illustrates this idea for a wealthy family.[2] The family's capitalized net spending rate is shown as an implied liability that must be subtracted from total assets to derive discretionary wealth. The ratio of assets to discretionary wealth, L, is the implicit leverage (noted as 2.6) that determines how conservative the investor needs to be to realize best long-term median results while avoiding the shortfall point.

This "discretionary wealth" approach to mean–variance optimization also implies a risk-control discipline for investors who experience large losses that they do not think they will soon recoup. That is, the method forces increased conservatism as the portfolio value approaches the shortfall point. Used this way, the process for updating risk aversion is akin to constant proportion portfolio insurance (CPPI) but with the critical difference that, given an already determined leverage, risk aversion is managed at a level that optimizes expected growth away from the shortfall point.[3]

---

[2]This approach is developed further in Chapter 3.

[3]A CPPI strategy basically buys shares as they rise and sells shares as they fall based on a floor the investor sets below which the portfolio is not allowed to fall. The floor increases in value at the rate of return on cash. The difference between the assets and floor can be thought of as a cushion, so the CPPI decision rule is simply to keep the exposure to shares a constant multiple of the cushion. Usually, but not always, there is a constraint that the equity allocation not exceed 100 percent.

Figure 2.1.   Investor Balance Sheet

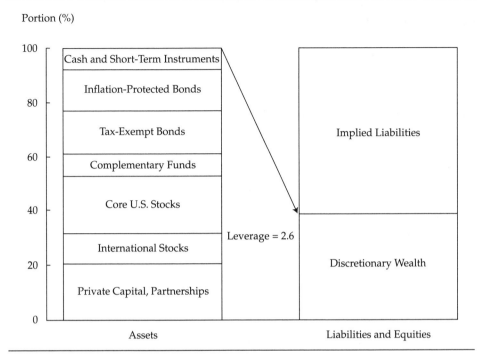

Summary

Financial theory oversimplifies the problems of private investors. It provides a starting point, but to be useful, it must be adapted carefully and extensively. The main ideas and adaptations are as follows:

- Most ideas and data available to the public are already well priced, which makes picking stocks, timing markets, and picking good managers problematic for most investors. This situation increases the relative importance of risk and tax management. Investors face a trade-off between risk and return, but specifying it for private investors through utility theory, which is idealized and relates to a single period, is often impractical.
- Markowitz mean–variance optimization is the best tool we have for balancing risk and return efficiently, but its correct implementation requires careful study.
- Option valuation theory teaches us that the choice of when to realize a taxable gain or loss is valuable and is enhanced by dispersion in returns and ratios of market value to cost basis.
- Stochastic growth theory helps us understand how to correctly balance return and risk to achieve long-term goals without triggering shortfalls along the way.

3. Life-Cycle Investing

Should investors have different portfolios when they are young, in middle age, and old? Should one's life-cycle pattern of asset allocations depend on how wealthy one is? Do a person's plans for disposition of wealth at the end of life make any difference? Intuition suggests that the answer to each of these questions is "yes," but investors and investment advisors need to be able to quantify these effects. The purpose of this chapter is to provide a structured and quantitative approach to answering these questions.

Although investment advisors may have their personal, subjective opinions, as advisors, they do not have a professional basis for telling clients how they should trade off current spending against future wealth. Advisors can, however, use simulations to show clients the possible distributions of outcomes under various assumptions about savings, spending, and possible investment results. Such simulations are best constructed period by period, with assumptions that reflect the best investment allocations the investment professional can construct for each point in the life cycle and contingent on the results to that point.

The key element in applying best-practice simulations is the *time series of implied balance sheets* (refer to Figure 2.1 in the previous chapter) showing the relationship of discretionary wealth to assets. Discretionary wealth is what is left over after implied and tangible financial assets have been added and after implied and tangible financial liabilities have been subtracted.[4] In this context, "discretionary" implies "what the investor would not like to give up but the loss of which would not be considered disastrous." The sequence of balance sheets, including the evolution in the implied leverage on discretionary wealth, is used period by period for asset allocation decisions. The review of evolving leverage should lead to better informed decisions—whether they are made qualitatively or quantitatively through mean–variance optimization. As the investor goes from youth to maturity to middle age to retirement to old age, the ratio of discretionary wealth to total assets will determine appropriate levels of investment aggressiveness.

Interaction of Life Cycle and Wealth

As a first cut, **Exhibit 3.1** shows a broad (there are many exceptions to it) characterization of typical best policies by wealth class and age. Note especially the *interaction* between age and wealth, which together are the key factors for an appropriate investment posture.

---

[4]See Chapter 4 for discussion of gradations in discretionary wealth.

Exhibit 3.1. Typical Best Policies by Stage and Wealth Class

Wealth Class	Young	Middle Age	Old
Very wealthy	Aggressive	Aggressive	Aggressive
High net worth	Balanced	Aggressive	Balanced/aggressive
Prosperous	Conservative	Balanced	Conservative
The rest of us	Conservative	Conservative	Very conservative

A surprise might be the conservative entries in the "young" column. The negative present value of a retirement spending stream liability plus possible liabilities for housing, children's college, and so on, may keep discretionary wealth low or negative until employment-related implied assets and financial assets build up. Then, the investor can make the transition from a conservative to a balanced strategy or from a balanced to an aggressive investment strategy. Many people, "the rest of us" row, may never accumulate enough discretionary wealth, even including implied assets from employment, to move beyond conservative or very conservative ideal portfolios.

Perhaps most investors would be classed as "prosperous." Also, those who are classed initially as high-net-worth (HNW) investors but later do poorly with their investments will need a second evolution in asset allocation (i.e., back to greater conservatism) as they move from employment and net savings to retirement and net spending. Unless they save significantly and have favorable investment returns, coupled with a restrained standard of living in retirement, these HNW investors will find their ratios of discretionary wealth to assets declining.

For those other HNW investors who do well with their investments, the situation may be quite different. Investors who significantly increase their proportion of discretionary assets to total wealth as they approach retirement (or even the end of life) can become more aggressive. This conclusion is contrary to the usual textbook recommendation (and also to the old saw that the equity allocation percentage should be 100 minus the investor's age), but it may be appropriate if investment prospects are likely to result in more wealth than will be needed over the investors' lives.

The extremely wealthy, shown in the top row of Exhibit 3.1, can usually maintain discretionary wealth at high levels for their entire lifetime and can always invest aggressively.

A time-sequenced set of balance sheets has far greater value for life-cycle customization if it includes not only conventional investments and debts but also *implied* assets and liabilities. Consider the general case: On the negative side, the present value of the implied liability for spending in retirement has a relatively modest value when one is young because of time discounting (and perhaps because of limited early lifestyle aspirations). It usually rises to a peak close to retirement and then may gradually diminish as future life expectancy shortens. On the positive side, implied employment assets (i.e., the present value of future savings during employment) build up through time and then diminish as retirement approaches.

To make the concept of employment-related implied assets clearer, **Figure 3.1** shows the implied balance sheet for a newly HNW executive in his mid-30s. He is not yet truly wealthy, but he has considerable implied wealth from employment. The wealth is composed of unvested stock and stock options plus the capitalization of his stream of savings during employment—all discounted not only with respect to time but for the ongoing probability of loss of employment. For simplicity, Figure 3.1 omits the valuation of life insurance and the implied liabilities for capital gains taxes.

Case Example

Juan inherits nothing but funding for a college education. He earns an engineering degree and a master's degree in business administration. Saving prudently, he gradually increases his saving rate as his salary and bonuses increase. His implied employment assets (i.e., the present value of his future savings during employment) also build up through time. By age 34, and based on his current lifestyle, Juan believes he has his minimum current retirement goals covered. To keep the example simple, assume that Juan never marries and will have no children. He carries minimal life insurance. (These simplifications allow this discussion to avoid the complicated issue of valuing life insurance, which has little value to Juan.)

Figure 3.1. New High-Net-Worth Investor's Balance Sheet

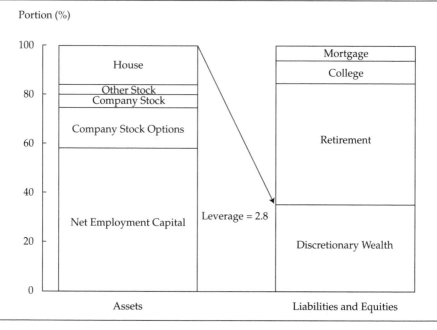

Figure 3.2 shows the paths of Juan's employment assets and retirement liabilities, together with more conventional investment assets, from age 20 to age 85. His capitalized savings stream from future employment continues to rise until he is 55. From that point until retirement at age 65, his implied employment assets decline as the savings period shortens. Because of prudent savings, aided by moderate investment performance, however, his financial assets rise steadily and, by his retirement, are larger than his implied employment assets.

After 55, Juan's financial assets continue to grow for some years but with much greater fluctuation than previously—for two reasons. First, growth of his financial assets (shown in Figure 3.2 after taxes and after inflation) is now dominated by investment returns rather than new savings. Second, his increased discretionary wealth permits all of his financial wealth to be invested in an equity portfolio rather than in less-volatile investments. Between age 55 and age 65, he does experience a rapidly *declining* present value of future employment, together with a rapidly *rising* present value of capitalized retirement spending (assuming a life expectancy of 85 years), which combine to bring discretionary wealth down from a peak of more than $2.5 million to a little less than $1.5 million in constant dollars.

Figure 3.2. Hypothetical Real Balance Sheet Series

Retired with no dependents, Juan sticks to his original prudent retirement lifestyle of spending an average of $250,000 after taxes and inflation for the next 20 years. He mentally sets aside a significant sum for medical expenses in the last years of his life. His investments gradually decline with his withdrawals from about $4.8 million to about $2.8 million. He leaves his estate to charity.

The key determinant of portfolio policy for Juan was the ratio of discretionary wealth to total assets. **Figure 3.3** shows how Juan's well-considered investment allocations evolved during his life on the basis of changes in this ratio. From age 20 through 33, the present value of Juan's retirement spending plan is greater than his total assets, even including the present value of future savings capitalized. In working out the investment returns during this period, the example assumes that because Juan is facing a shortfall relative to the present value of money needed for retirement, he allocates no money to stocks until discretionary wealth becomes positive. A different investor might think that any losses on the stock market could be made up by a contingent increased rate of savings, but Juan does not feel that he has that flexibility. (Valuing flexibility is discussed in the next section.)

Figure 3.3. Hypothetical Ratio of Discretionary Wealth to Total Assets

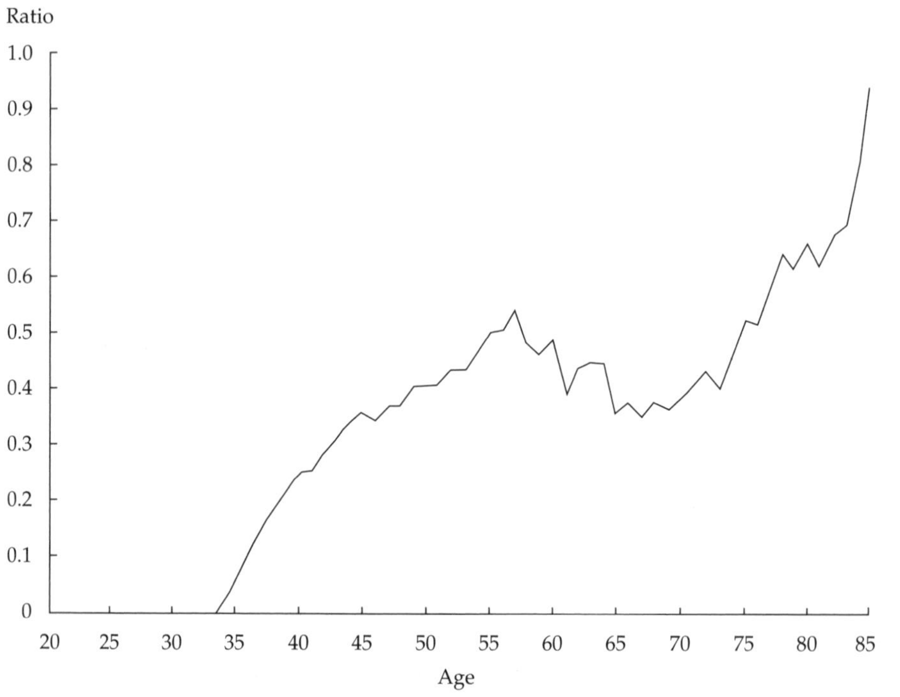

From age 34 to age 56, Juan gradually increases his allocation to equities, with 100 percent allocation during his peak prosperity in terms of discretionary wealth as a fraction of total assets. This period is before the present value of his retirement liability begins to be important. Juan favors actively managed funds, and for simplicity, the assumption is that, on average, he has no unrealized capital gains or losses each year.

After a peak in discretionary wealth relative to prosperity in middle age, Juan becomes a bit more conservative; he retreats to a balanced stock/bond portfolio as the present value of his remaining employment declines and the present value of retirement spending increases. After about age 75, however, he realizes that his investment returns are more than keeping up with the gradually declining present value of his retirement spending. That is, with his increasing age, his fraction of discretionary wealth to total assets begins increasing again as the present value of retirement spending begins to shrink. In other words, Juan is not likely to outlive his funds and he has no fixed obligations. This development allows funds to once again be invested in an aggressive portfolio, although one from which he can receive adequate cash flow.

This example shows how good investment policy can change over an investor's life cycle. It is clear that a rule of thumb such as "the percentage of equity should be equal to 100 minus the investor's age" will not generally work for many HNW (and most all very wealthy) investors, who may be able to handle even more risk as they get older. For the other end of the age spectrum, there is a strong argument that those young people with little wealth and without the flexibility to increase their savings if investments turn sour should be very conservative. More generally, the oft-touted virtues of the stock market do not apply to those with few financial resources, even though long-run *average* returns of stocks are indeed higher than long-run bond returns. Those on the edge of financial disaster cannot afford to take much risk.

Flexibility of Employment Earnings and Consumption Spending

What happens if discretionary wealth falls to zero or even becomes negative? People in this situation have to readjust their thinking—even if it is painful—about what they must earn or can spend. The desirability of flexibility in employment earnings, consumption, and financial requirements means that portfolio investment is actually a subproblem within a broader set of choices that, if considered in complete detail, would involve complicated mathematics.

To simplify the investment problem, however, rather than make it more complex, the investment advisor might show a wealthy investor who initially requires capitalizing $1 million a year in a spending allowance that perhaps, in an emergency, he or she could live on less, perhaps 80 percent of that amount. Then, the 20 percent difference can be capitalized as a flexibility asset by discounting it not only for time but also for the subjectively estimated probability that this flexibility will actually be used. Having flexibility among future employment, consumption, and savings has a quasi-option value that, in itself, is a type of asset. Rather than ignoring flexibility, when it is material relative to discretionary wealth, the advisor can take it into account as an asset-like feature. Treatment of flexibility as a crudely valued option asset oversimplifies a complex situation, but it is better than leaving flexibility out of the investment plan altogether.

Because large and sudden shocks to consumption are painful, arriving at a given increment of discretionary wealth by saving small amounts over long periods is much easier than arriving by saving large amounts over a short period. *Flexibility favors the young investor because it allows him or her to be more aggressive in allocation to stocks and other risky assets.* Nevertheless, this protection is limited, and the default position should be that young investors of limited means and heavy financial responsibilities should be conservative.

Remaining Lifetime Risks

Outliving one's assets may not be a concern for the very wealthy, but it is a pressing concern to investors of moderate wealth, even some who would be classified as HNW investors. The investment that addresses the risk of outliving one's savings is an annuity.

The question of whether an annuity is appropriate for a client depends on both life situation and price. Whether annuities are overpriced depends not only on provider profits and costs for marketing but also on tax issues. For example, in the United States, the taxation of distributions from annuities is figured by subtracting the original contribution of principal, and then, on the negative side, all gains are taxed at ordinary income tax rates. One does not get the benefit of lower capital gains tax rates. On the positive side, annuities provide the benefits of genuine risk pooling. For high-tax-bracket individuals, and with the currently low U.S. dividend and capital gains tax rates, one can argue that self-insurance through investing is competitive with annuities.

Without something like an annuity, how can the investor best manage the risk arising from an uncertain remaining life span? The investor could, from the beginning, plan for a longer life than actuarially expected. That approach would build in an additional safety cushion by reducing discretionary wealth. Alternatively (or additionally), the investor could incorporate life expectancy risk in mean–variance optimization by treating the retirement liability as a short position with a risky return that reflects variation in present value through time as one discounts possible longer or shorter periods. Because this risk is not a hedge against some positive asset return risk, it will make the investor more conservative. *Uncertainty about length of life is properly reflected in a more conservative investment portfolio.*[5]

Disposition of Excess Wealth

Wealth transfers involving gifts and estates is the domain of experts in tax law, but once the alternatives have been identified, they can be analyzed in the framework put forward in this chapter. The after-tax cash flow streams can be reduced to implied and explicit assets and liabilities, and the resulting sequence of balance sheets and their implications for asset allocation by location can be analyzed in a Markowitz mean–variance framework.

Even if the investor should have little faith in, or ability to implement, a full-fledged algorithmic solution to planning disposition of wealth, the effort to put the problem into the sequence of implied balance sheets will lead to a firmer grasp of the nature of the decisions he or she needs to make.

Summary

Combining stochastic growth theory with the notion of avoiding interim shortfalls leads us to a framework for

- managing discretionary wealth as the key to avoiding shortfalls and achieving long-term financial goals and
- expanding the investor's balance sheet to include implied liabilities, such as capitalized retirement, lifestyle maintenance, and taxes for unrealized capital gains, and to include implied assets, such as capitalized employment-related savings and unvested benefits.

The resulting framework for financial planning, which should be contingent on both age and financial outcomes, guides life-cycle investing, which involves

- summarizing current optimal risk attitudes in the ratio of assets to discretionary wealth,
- subjecting plans to a disciplined review and revision as discretionary wealth and the investment environment change, and
- clarifying the need to address flexibility, end-of-life risk reduction, and plans for excess wealth disposition.

---

[5]We do not discuss in this book the present value of life insurance, but a market is developing for life insurance policies, from which the prices give some idea of the policies' present monetary value. That measure may not do justice, however, to the complementarity of life insurance to a family's employment assets, where life insurance functions in a way not dissimilar to a put option on continued employment consequences.

Part II
Private Wealth and Taxation

In this part, the chapters aim to convey the viewpoint of the wealthy investor toward financial matters. What matter most, at least in comparison with institutional investors, are taxation and provisions for transferring wealth to others. Chapter 4 is a general description of attitudes and circumstances. Chapter 5 describes in considerable detail how the U.S. tax code affects the wealthy investor, with particular attention to capital gains taxes and the estate tax. Chapter 6 describes important strategies for improving after-tax returns.

4. Lifestyle, Wealth Transfer, and Asset Classes

In the late 1950s, one of the most popular shows on television was "The Millionaire." Each episode was a short story in which an emissary, Michael Anthony, delivered to an unsuspecting recipient a $1 million check from John Beresford Tipton, an eccentric multimillionaire. For the recipient, this gift was a dramatic, life-changing event, for better or for worse, like sweeping a state lottery is today.

Half a century later, millionaires are commonplace and billionaires are common enough to fill more than two-thirds of the Forbes 400 list, which surely undercounts the actual number. Such is the result of a combination of inflation, general growth in wealth (at least in nominal terms), and a change in the distribution of wealth, with an increasing concentration at the upper ranges.

According to the World Wealth Report 2005 published by Merrill Lynch and Capgemini, more than 8 million people had assets greater than $1 million, excluding their primary residences, in 2004. The report categorized this wealth as high-net-worth (HNW) individuals ($1 million to $5 million), midtier millionaires ($5 million to $30 million), and ultra-HNW individuals (more than $30 million). It estimated that worldwide the numbers are 7,445,800 HNW individuals, 774,800 midtier millionaires, and 77,500 ultra-HNW individuals. Although the category limits are somewhat subjective, note that each higher category has roughly a tenth the number of people in the category below it.

Wealth of the HNW Household

U.S. Internal Revenue Service (IRS) statistics show that the top 10 percent threshold of adjusted gross income (AGI) for 2002 was $92,663.[6] The top 1 percent threshold of AGI was $285,424, which was 10 times the median AGI. Federal income tax filers of more than $1 million of AGI, which is the top 0.13 percent, numbered 168,608.

According to 1997 data, the top 1 percent of households holds approximately 30 percent of all the wealth in the United States, and the top 5 percent holds about 55 percent of all the wealth (Quadrini and Rios-Rull 1997). Using 1998 data from the Federal Reserve's Survey of Consumer Finances, Montalto (2001) reported that

---

[6]"Tax Stats at a Glance: Summary of Collections before Refunds by Type of Return, FY 2003." For these statistics and information on all federal taxes in this chapter, see www.irs.gov.

4.5 percent of U.S. households at that time, about 4.6 million, had assets, including their primary residences, of $1 million or more. More than 80 percent of these HNW (greater than $1 million) households were headed by someone at least 45 years old. For the HNW group, financial assets (e.g., cash, stocks, bonds, mutual funds) and nonfinancial assets (e.g., real estate and business interests) each constitute about half (mean share) of the net assets. The World Wealth Report 2005 estimated that there are about 2.5 million people in the United States with assets, excluding their primary residences, greater than $1 million.

Investors with a financial net worth ranging from $1 million to $5 million, excluding primary residences, are typically limited to using mutual funds or directly owning public stocks and bonds. They have limited access to the kind of products, such as private equity, that institutions can use. Many will be somewhere in the upper ranges of tax rates, for both income and estate taxes.

The group from about $5 million to $30 million has the wherewithal to invest in stocks and bonds through individual accounts and to have some limited participation in alternative asset classes, mostly through expensive retail investment partnerships or some funds of hedge funds. The vast majority are likely to be in the top marginal tax brackets and are potentially subject to substantial estate tax. The trend is for families at the higher end of this range to work in multifamily offices to achieve the economy of scale necessary to have access to institutional advice and investment opportunities.

Families and individuals with more than $30 million in assets are likely to have some combination of family investment office, financial advisor, and sophisticated tax planner. This group will have varying mixes of concentrated direct investments and more diversified institutional kinds of investments. They also have enough liquid wealth to invest in most of the alternative asset classes, such as hedge funds, private equity, venture capital, and institutional real estate. Despite the typically unattractive tax treatment of hedge funds, hedge fund strategies (collectively) represent the most popular alternative asset classes for this group.

Families and individuals with more than $100 million start to look and act more like institutional investors. They often have their own family offices, with some investment professionals, and have access to the majority of institutional investment products, including such illiquid investments as private equity and venture capital partnerships. Their asset allocations and investment strategies are fully as sophisticated as those of most institutional investors. They can afford the best investment advice from institutional consultants and tax attorneys. They can rarely afford in-house money managers until their investment assets approach about $1 billion, however, in which case directly employing in-house managers for specific asset classes can become economical.

At the top end are those with wealth in the billions (even tens of billions). The Forbes 400 list for 2004 probably undercounts the number of mega-rich and underestimates the wealth reported, but even so, it lists *278 billionaires*. For the majority of billionaires (or billionaire families), wealth is often concentrated in directly owned or controlled businesses but substantial liquid wealth is left for other investments. These rare investors are highly individualized but typically function as institutional investors with respect to their diversified financial investments.

Whether the levels of wealth are *qualitatively* different is not clear, although common sense would suggest so. Perhaps jumps in functional wealth are characterized by a log function; perhaps increments such as $1 million, $10 million, $100 million, $1 billion, and $10 billion are useful wealth "plateaus" or categories. An alternative view is that a completely different functional relative-wealth plateau may be achieved when the annual return on the wealth approximates the total wealth of the category just below it. If such plateaus correctly characterize the relative desirability of wealth, this factor has obvious implications for the implied shape of the utility curve corresponding to each plateau. In contrast to these wealth/utility categorizations, an investment-oriented categorization of wealth might take into account the widening choices of asset classes and investment vehicles that become practical and available as wealth levels increase. (Wealth levels as they relate to categories of consumption are discussed indirectly in the next section.)

With the range of wealth so extreme, identifying and discussing the "average" HNW investor is difficult. The goals, needs, and financial aspirations of the diverse but small number of HNW investors vary widely (much more than for those in or below the upper middle class, where more homogenous financial circumstances are the norm). But one thing the HNW all have in common is that taxes have a significant effect on their ability to retain and increase their wealth.

Consumption, Spending, and Risk Management

For most people, spending and consumption are essentially the same thing, but for the very wealthy, consumption is usually much less than total spending. Their basic needs for consumption—that is, clothing, food, shelter, and so on—are easily met and exceeded. For the very wealthy, even luxury wants are easily satisfied. A portion of their spending in excess of consumption is devoted to a variety of expensive consumer durables—luxury housing, second homes, yachts, airplanes, works of art, high-end jewelry. These expenditures are highly discretionary and are related to investment returns, but they are not necessarily *consumption*, at least not in amount equal to the expenditure. Pointing to the highly discretionary nature of luxury spending, Ait-Sahalia, Parker, and Yogo (2004) found, "By contrast [with basic goods] the consumption of luxuries is both more volatile and more correlated with excess [stock market] returns" (p. 2961). In fact, some nonconsumption expenditures on goods such as homes or works of art may even appreciate and have the potential to create an inflation hedge. For the extremely wealthy, to completely dissipate one's wealth by spending is hard.

In assessing an HNW client's risk tolerance, the important difference between total spending and consumption should be explicitly recognized in terms of how much risk can be tolerated. The following simple categorization of spending needs and desires is an aid in this assessment:

1. Basic necessities (food, basic housing, basic clothing, utilities, transportation, medical/insurance coverage)
2. Lifestyle maintenance (education, entertainment, dining out, child care, family vacations)
3. Luxury consumption (luxury travel, luxury clothes, domestic staff, luxury furnishings)
4. Noninvestment assets (luxury primary home, second home, yacht, private airplane, art, antiques)
5. Savings and investments (bank accounts, employee stock and options, pensions, whole life insurance, stocks, bonds, alternative investments)

A sixth category, which is not as rare as one might think, is the goal of making money as an end in itself, either for ego, prestige, or a sense of "winning."

Most of these elements must be funded with *after-tax money*. Expenditures require cash. Many clients and advisors become confused by thinking that *income* is required to maintain lifestyle. In fact, cash is the medium for purchasing goods and services, and cash is not identical with income. Income—consisting of salary, interest, and dividends—is taxed either heavily (salary and interest) or moderately (dividends) and may not be the most tax-efficient way to fund expenditures. In some instances, taxable income is generated that has no accompanying cash ("phantom income") as when a partnership has taxable income but does not distribute cash.

Today, to the extent that investments provide the main source for expenditures, capital appreciation and dividends are among the most effective methods of generating cash.[7] Sales of securities at or below cost can generate cash with no current tax at all. Distinguishing the need for cash rather than "income" will help an advisor craft an optimal investment program.

Shortfall Constraints

The topic of shortfall constraints for institutional investors, most of which are tax exempt, has been well developed by Leibowitz (1992). The immunization of liabilities through asset matching is another topic that has been well developed for the tax-exempt investor. For the majority of individuals, who spend most of what they earn, these concepts have little application because their savings are too limited to provide resources for asset/liability matching or immunization; moreover, they

---

[7]This has become true only recently in the United States; until 2003 when Congress lowered the tax on dividends to 15 percent, dividends were extremely tax inefficient.

often have financial liabilities but little in the way of financial assets. For the HNW investor, however, a tax-adjusted adaptation of these institutional techniques will be of value in securing the financial well being of the investor and family.

For private investors, the advisor has to take into account not only the magnitude and probability of a shortfall but also the personal *importance* (personal negative utility) of the shortfall. This problem is different from the situation facing most tax-exempt investors. They are concerned with shortfalls measured in dollars to match known liabilities and little concerned with large differences in marginal utility. For most individuals, such differences are important: Not being able to make a child's college tuition payment is very different from not being able to trade in a 100-foot yacht for a 150-foot yacht. An advisor could develop shortfall-constraint analyses separately for each expenditure category—for example, the five categories listed previously.

Because many of the "liabilities" of the wealthy investor are related to consumption—in particular, the "conspicuous consumption" described by Veblen (1994)—they may not be easily deferred without unpleasant disruptions in lifestyle. So, the ability to weather temporary reductions in investment wealth, investment-related income, or salary income may be more than a dollar-and-cents issue. For the highly discretionary categories of expenditures, the importance of a temporary reduction should be less than for more basic needs. Adequate risk analysis needs to take into account the consequences as well as the likelihood and magnitude of the potential loss. Permanent losses of wealth can have emotional consequences, as well as economic consequences, that adversely affect self-esteem and social prestige.

In modeling or analyzing taxable portfolios, especially in light of shortfall constraints, the advisor needs to be aware of some peculiar potential tax implications. Portfolios with poor performance will usually have proportionately more losses than gains. Thus, the opportunity to offset losses with gains within or outside these investment portfolios may be limited or nonexistent. Conventional approaches to modeling after-tax returns usually give full credit to tax losses, but poorly performing portfolios may not allow the use of these losses, in which case, conventional estimates of the tax benefits are overstated. Unusable losses create a tax asymmetry whereby portfolios with net losses are functionally pretax and thus larger than the equivalent tax-exempt portfolios, but portfolios with net gains are after tax and thus smaller than the equivalent tax-exempt portfolios. In other words, portfolio analysis should be based on effective, not nominal, tax rates, which may be idiosyncratic to the circumstances of the specific investor.

Shrinking (Finite) Time Horizons

As investors get older, their investment horizons shrink, which has important investment and tax implications. The *actuarial* life expectancy is not fixed at birth but is conditional upon having reached greater age, so the life expectancy of a person at age 10 is less than that of a person who has reached age 60. Obviously, *life span*—that is, the maximum length of life—has a practical upper limit; life span is not infinite, but nonetheless, a person who outlives the actuarial tables and runs out of money has a serious problem. Consequently, planning needs to take into account the longest possible survival, not actuarial life expectancy alone. Conventional actuarial practice is to forecast life expectancy *on average for large sets of people*, which can be done with high accuracy. With a sample size of one individual, the average life expectancy is simply the wrong measure of what people have to worry about.

The average investor's risk tolerance may decrease as life span and investment horizon decrease, but very wealthy investors with bequest goals for their wealth may have an increasing risk tolerance because they are not investing for consumption during their own lifetimes but, rather, to bequeath money to charities or subsequent generations. In the case of a surviving spouse, particularly one who is substantially younger than the investor, the problem can be thought of as an extended life expectancy of the investor.

When the investment horizon becomes shorter as a consequence of shorter life expectancy, the rational course of action for most investors is to minimize the recognition of taxable gains. The gains will almost always incur less tax at death than during a person's lifetime, with the remaining value of the investment assets left for the estate tax. The asset mix should reflect not only any end-of-life changes in risk tolerance, but also the tremendous advantages of tax deferral and the potential to avoid tax entirely for estates below the threshold for estate tax exemption.[8]

The estate tax applies, if at all, to the fair market value, which is the sum of the tax basis plus all unrecognized gains, although there are some differences between the treatment of private investments and the treatment of publicly traded securities. (Private investments are another matter because of the possibility of discounts from gross fair market value based on factors such as illiquidity, minority discounts, and restrictions on transferability.) At the time of death, any unrecognized capital gains escape capital gains tax, but the amount of the unrecognized gain is part of the estate assets subject to the estate tax.

The amount saved by not realizing gains during the investor's lifetime is calculated as

$$(1 - \text{Estate tax rate}) \times (\text{Unrealized gain} \times \text{Capital gains tax rate}).$$

For other types of estate planning (e.g., leaving money to one's spouse), the tax-deferral period can be enhanced, which adds value.

---

[8] As of fall 2005, the estate tax applies only to estates of more than $1,500,000, and this threshold is expected to rise.

The Estate Tax and Wealth Transfer

Although the topic of estate planning is complex, extensive, and outside the scope of this monograph, some important points need to be made because the goal of many investment programs for HNW investors includes leaving wealth to family members, charities, and others. The estate tax and the gift tax are every bit as much a tax on investments as are income and capital gains taxes but are given little attention in the investment literature.

The estate tax potentially applies to approximately the wealthiest 2 percent of taxable households in the United States. Some estate planners have called it the only "voluntary" tax in the United States, meaning that people have so many ways to avoid paying estate tax that an estate is relatively rarely subject to it. Although this statement is true to an extent, the estate tax applies to a significant portion of the HNW population. Small estates may incur no estate tax at all, and a step-up in basis to fair market value at time of death means that a subsequent sale at the same fair market value has no capital gain. Thus, investments with unrealized gains held until death are functionally tax exempt. One of the many oddities of the tax law is that individuals with estates that are not above the exemption receive much better tax treatment at death than when the investor was alive; at death, all the potential tax liability on unrecognized gains is completely wiped away forever.

The tax law is favorable for transfers of assets between spouses. Assets can be transferred to a spouse during life or at death with no immediate tax implication. This aspect creates an important opportunity for tax deferral. The probability function of joint survivorship of a married couple is different from the actuarial life expectancy of either spouse alone; joint actuarial life is longer. Therefore, the investment planning horizon can be far longer than the earliest-to-die estimate of a married couple. Assets left to a spouse, either directly or through a trust (e.g., a qualified terminal income property trust), need not be taxed until the death of the surviving spouse. Modeling across the investment horizon needs to take these path dependencies into account because they have serious tax implications and thereby affect after-tax returns and terminal wealth.

By adding many years to potential tax deferral, the advantageous differential between pretax and after-tax compounding, discussed in Chapter 6, can be dramatically enhanced. When combined with the estate tax exemption, this potential may allow a substantial pool of untaxed investment assets. The estate tax exemption for each spouse still applies, but any assets in excess of the first-to-die exemption will carry over at the decedent's cost basis.

Horvitz and Wilcox (2003) showed that the mechanism of tax deferral is differential compounding; the difference between pretax and after-tax terminal wealth is a nonlinear function of time and the differential in pretax and after-tax compounding rates. Leaving investment assets untaxed to a surviving spouse extends the time for that compounding difference, often for many years, and at the same time provides a larger base for interest and/or dividends for current income.

Investors with children often wish to provide support to them during the investor's lifetime and with a bequest upon death. Under current tax treatment, the gift tax during the investor's life is always less expensive than the estate tax for the same dollars transferred because the tax on gifts applies to the amount transferred whereas the estate tax is paid on the gross amount, leaving only the net available for transfer.[9] With a gift, however, the investor does give up control of the funds and the right to use the money. To transfer $100,000 net as a gift at a 50 percent gift tax rate requires $150,000 pretax, whereas the same $100,000 transferred from a taxable estate at the same rate requires $200,000. Appreciated property transferred by gift does not receive a step-up in basis. If sold at a gain by the transferee, tax is due on the difference between the donor's basis and what is received on sale; if sold at a loss, the difference is the lesser of the difference between the donor's basis and (1) the sale price or (2) the fair market value at the time of transfer.

Another option is to separate assets into "artificial" components, such as a "life estate" and "remainder." The life estate is computed as an actuarial function based on the investor's presumed lifetime and a statutory discount rate that creates a present value for tax purposes; the difference is the remainder interest. If the investment assets can earn more than the discount rate, the net value will accrue without additional gift or estate tax. Such techniques have implications for the kinds of assets to be partitioned into the life and remainder interests. For example, one technique is to retain a life interest in an investment with a high expected return while making a gift or sale of the remainder interest and valuing the life interest by using the applicable federal rate, which is set by the IRS and reflects low-risk rates of return. The excess return from the actual investment will accrue to the remainder interest. There are many variations of these apportionments.

The techniques for handling gifts and bequests are too varied and complex to cover in this monograph, but readers should understand the availability of ways to minimize current tax treatment—and possibly avoid it entirely. Planning for spousal and intergenerational transfers should be made part of any investment program and should take into account the tax treatment of funds upon transfer or disposition, asset location (discussed in Chapter 9), and the implication of tax deferral for periods extending beyond the investment horizon of the investor.

Complete investment planning means integrating family assets—the assets held by the investor, the investor's parents (if an inheritance is anticipated), the spouse, and the investor's children. It means taking into account the time horizons for each of these family members. For optimal integration of investment planning, the advisor should consider locating specific types of assets in the hands of certain family members while regarding the entire portfolio as an integrated, diversified whole.

---

[9] For the mathematics, see Horvitz and Wilcox.

For investors who intend to make charitable bequests, proper tax management can result in investment returns approaching those of tax-exempt investors. The reason is simple: To the extent that investment gains are deferred upon death or *inter vivos* disposition, they are never taxed, which effectively results in a tax-free return. This effect is true whether the investor/descendant makes the bequest or whether the assets are left to a spouse who then makes the bequest. Investors who intend to donate substantial amounts of their wealth to charity should be particularly sensitive to the value of tax deferral and tax-managed investing to maximize the effective rate of return and the terminal value of the assets to be transferred. Investors who make donations during their lifetime benefit from a deduction equal to the fair market values, so lifetime donations of highly appreciated securities are an effective alternative to bequests; they eliminate capital gains while providing a potential deduction against high-rate ordinary income. Donations do reduce wealth but not dollar for dollar—which can be another reason to maximize tax deferral.

Case Example

Mary, a divorced 50-year-old living in upstate New York, inherits a trust of some $2 million cash from her parents; it supplements the $350,000-a-year salary she earns as a corporate executive. Mary saves part of her salary income and part of her trust distributions for her children. The trust is administered by a professional bank trust department as trustee. The terms of the trust are that Mary is to receive the greater of (1) all the distributable net income or (2) 5 percent of the asset value for life, with the remainder to be held in trust for the benefit of her two children and further descendants when she dies.

The bank assigns a trust administration officer and an investment officer to the account. The trustee decides on a conventional asset allocation of 60 percent stocks and 40 percent bonds. The trustee's investment department has a list of about 100 stocks from the S&P 500 Index that it follows and approves for the trust accounts, but the investment officers have discretion to vary the proportions of the specific security holdings. The assigned investment officer generally follows the standard stock list and buys and sells stocks to stay with that list. The bond portfolio is a diversified selection of New York state municipal bonds. All these decisions appear to be prudent and unassailable by fiduciary standards.

Unfortunately, Mary's income makes her subject to the alternative minimum tax (AMT), so the nominal coupon from the municipal bonds produces less income after taxes than she would have received if she had been invested in higher-yielding taxable bonds. If the investment officer had used higher-yielding taxable bonds, some of the AMT effect could have been mitigated. The trustee has failed to consider Mary's tax situation outside the trust factors and simply assumed that tax-exempt bonds are better than taxable bonds for high-bracket taxpayers. Next, municipal issuers in New York experience financial difficulties that cause the municipal bonds to drop in credit rating and in value. The trustee has focused solely on the tax exemption in Mary's state of domicile (to keep the exemption for state tax purposes) and failed to diversify these municipal bond holdings. Moreover, the stock strategy he has selected is subject to turnover as the recommended list changes, which eliminates any real value for tax deferral.

Because of the high annual recognition of capital gains and the payout of municipal income instead of taxable income (which would have been nominally more), the life-estate interest is favored over the remainder interest, so the remainder interest diminishes more than anticipated and more than either Mary or her parents would have wanted. Because the trust is under the generation-skipping transfer tax exemption, no estate tax will be due on the death of Mary or her descendants, which makes the remainder interest extremely valuable from an estate tax perspective and is consistent with Mary's (and her parents') goals of leaving money to the next generation without estate tax. The trustee has been wasting this valuable opportunity.

By failing to take into account Mary's total tax picture as integrated with the trust, the trustee has ignored her intentions for saving for her children and their children. By focusing on simplistic tax management and working from the premise of what the trust department "usually does" (instead of what Mary needs), the trustee is, in fact, doing a poor job while still looking professional.

Gross-to-Net Investment Returns

Gross investment returns must absorb four key factors if they are to provide long-term purchasing power. The factors are the "Four Horsemen of the Investment Apocalypse" that can devastate purchasing power:

1. investment expenses (for example, management fees, transaction and custody costs),
2. taxes (income and estate taxes),
3. inflation, and
4. consumption.

Consumption, the ultimate purpose of wealth accumulation for most people, must come after the first three factors are satisfied. More than anything else, the long-term erosion of purchasing power (which is the functional definition of wealth) is the most serious problem for the HNW investor faced with the interplay of taxation and inflation.

Investment Expenses. The tax rules can be complex with respect to deducting investment expenses. Generally, direct transaction costs (e.g., commissions) and indirect transaction costs (e.g., the market impact of trading) reduce the net gain that will be taxed. Manager fees may have various tax treatments; they can reduce capital gains or, in some instances, result in a deduction against ordinary income because itemized deductions are subject to limits as a percentage of adjusted gross income. The effect is to increase the marginal tax rate approximately in the amount of the percentage limitation.

Manager fees are almost always a percentage of assets under management and their effect on net returns is easily calculated by subtracting the fee rate from the gross rate of return. Transaction costs are much harder to identify, but they are mostly a function of activity (i.e., turnover). High levels of activity can seriously reduce gross return, yet individuals commonly pay little attention to turnover. In fact, many investors would be appalled at paying a manager a fee for "doing nothing," even if it is the best thing to do.

Impact of Taxation and Inflation. For investments to preserve purchasing power, they have to return more than the inflation rate *after* deducting management fees, costs, and taxes. Using U.S. tax rates applicable at the time (not today's rates) and actual inflation rates for 1925–2004, Ibbotson Associates (2005) found the compound annual returns, net of taxes and inflation for that period, for the U.S. asset classes shown in **Table 4.1**.[10]

Table 4.1. Annualized Compound Returns, 1925–2004
(net of taxes and inflation)

U.S. Asset	Return
Stocks	4.8%
Municipal bonds	1.3
Government bonds	0.8
Treasury bills	−0.9

Source: Ibbotson Associates (2005).

The difference for the Ibbotson data between the long-term pretax, preinflation returns and after-tax, postinflation annualized returns was about 4.5 percent for bonds and about 5.4 percent for stocks. For taxable investors, one may reasonably ask whether their "long run" will be long enough to reliably use static percentage asset allocations to bonds when faced with taxes and inflation and the possibility of multidecade periods of loss.

■ *Fixed income.* The U.S. bond markets, adjusted for taxes and inflation rates existing at the time of the study reported in Table 4.1, show extremely long trends of gaining and losing purchasing power—trends that go for decades. A growth of

---

10These results would be very different, and more attractive, if the analysis used today's tax rates, which are some of the lowest seen in the post–World War II era.

net purchasing power went on for about 20 years from 1925 until the beginning of World War II, followed by about 35 years of loss in net purchasing power. This remarkable loss of value was then followed by the great bond bull market from the early 1980s to the present, which nearly tripled the net purchasing power of long-term (more than 20 years) bondholders. These long trending effects on net purchasing power are the result of the confluence of market conditions, inflation eras, and tax regimes. No one factor completely accounts for the results. The conventional wisdom that taxable investors should *always* hold bonds as a permanent part of their investment portfolios—irrespective of expected returns, expected taxes, and expected inflation—should be questioned, especially for long-term wealthy investors.

Treasury Inflation-Indexed Securities (commonly called TIPS) provide inflation protection, but somewhat less than one might think because the inflation component is also taxed annually at high ordinary income rates. Thus, these securities are most suitable for tax-sheltered retirement accounts. Depending on the changing state of yields, inflation, and tax rates, TIPS may not always completely maintain purchasing power unless held in a tax-sheltered vehicle.

In Table 4.1, the long-term after-tax results for municipal bonds are slightly better than the results for U.S. government bonds, but diversification with municipal bonds can be difficult without going to bonds outside the state of residence of the investor, which eliminates the exemption for state tax purposes. A portfolio of single-state bonds is subject to much more risk than a multistate portfolio. Treasuries, taxed at the federal level, are not subject to any state or local income taxes, but normally yield less than bonds with lower credit ratings. Municipal bonds often come with call features that make them worth less than noncallable taxable bonds. They are also often more mispriced and expensive to trade than their taxable counterparts. The longer maturities of municipal bonds are often more attractive to taxable investors than is the short end of the market.

The permanent, strong diversification benefit of fixed-income investments is not always reliable; when bond returns are positively correlated with stocks for extended time periods, as during periods of high inflation, their diversification benefit is reduced. The place of fixed-income instruments, particularly long-dated bonds for wealthy investors with high proportions of discretionary wealth, must be carefully considered because of their potentially low after-tax returns, modest diversification benefits, and exposure to the erosion of purchasing power resulting from inflation.

■ *Stocks.* U.S. stocks have provided long-term protection of net purchasing power, but long periods have occurred when even stocks lost purchasing power for the taxable investor. Until the end of WWII, the stock market was characterized by jagged multiyear ups and downs with a long trend up in net purchasing power. From roughly the end of WWII until about the mid-1960s, the U.S. market experienced 20 years of mostly upward movement in net purchasing power. For about the next 20 years, a long trend of seriously diminished net purchasing power occurred. In fact, an investor in the S&P 500 in 1967 did not recover purchasing power until about 13 years later. The loss of purchasing power during that period, peak to trough, was about 25 percent. This period was followed by the great bull market beginning in the early 1980s that resulted in a stunning surge in net purchasing power.

The dividend component used to be unattractive to investors in high tax brackets, but with recent changes to the tax law, the return from stocks, whether from dividends or long-term capital gain, is taxed at the same rate. The remaining advantage of long-term capital gains is the potential for tax deferral.[11]

■ *Cash.* Although cash may sometimes be king, it does not provide a good hedge against inflation. Historically, T-bills have returned slightly above the inflation rate *pretax*, but because the return is taxed as ordinary income, T-bills will almost always return less than inflation after taxes. The result is a slow hemorrhaging in purchasing power that becomes unsustainable after long periods of time.

■ *Alternative asset classes.* Space does not allow more than a cursory treatment of the many other asset classes. (A somewhat fuller overview can be found in Chapter 5.) Most hedge funds engage in investment activities that are highly tax inefficient.

Most arbitrage strategies are inherently short term in nature and involve some degree of U.S. Internal Revenue Code Section 1256 contracts, in which taxes may not be deferred and which mandate tax allocation of gains to 60 percent long-term capital gains and 40 percent short-term capital gains. At today's rate, this requirement results in an effective federal tax rate of 23 percent. Hedge funds engaged in very active trading in long or short security strategies usually generate large proportions of short-term gain and loss, which usually have the worst kind of tax treatment. Private equity and venture capital generally have favorable tax treatment because the capital gains tend to be long term. In addition, certain fees and expenses (e.g., management fees) may be a deduction against ordinary income. Real estate is subject to a higher tax rate for long-term capital gains than are many other types of asset classes, although depreciation can shield current income. Unless the deferral period is long, however, the savings may not be important, especially because the depreciation must be recaptured at high tax rates. Hard assets such as timber, gold, oil, and gas have generally favorable tax characteristics. Timber is literally a growing asset, with the potential for relatively long tax deferral of gains that accrue and a depletion formula that temporarily shelters income. Oil and gas investments can have favorable depreciation and depletion deductions.

---

[11]In one of the curiosities of the tax code, interest is a deductible expense for corporations but dividends are not. From a total-value point of view, combining the tax paid by the corporation with the tax paid by the investor, interest payments may actually be better if the equity can be characterized as debt. But rules concerning thinly capitalized corporations prohibit extreme abuses. Dividend-paying corporations with either tax-exempt or taxable shareholders have a higher cost of capital than otherwise identical interest-paying corporations and should be worth less, even to taxable investors.

Access to the alternative investments is limited to the very wealthiest investors unless the investor uses intermediaries who, for a substantial fee, provide commingled investment vehicles for HNW investors in the lower wealth ranges. In analyzing funds of funds or other pooled conduits for investors who cannot meet the minimum investment requirements for direct access, the advisor needs to understand the impact of the overlay management fees and additional carried interest paid to the intermediary. In some cases, the fees, particularly the management fees, can eviscerate most of the financial advantages of the asset class.[12]

Other specialized products attempt to replicate the investment performance of an asset class, such as hedge funds, by using structured financial products. They pay a return based on the performance of a specialized index, much like conventional stock index futures, without a direct investment in the underlying assets, and they purportedly capture the systematic risk and return of the asset class. For example, the investor might enter into an arrangement to purchase a warrant that will pay the total return of a basket of hedge funds. Supposedly, the return will be treated as all long-term capital gains rather than a pass-through of income taxed at the higher rate that would have occurred had the investment been made directly in the hedge funds.

Such products and the indices on which they are based raise substantial concerns for the taxable investor. The details are beyond the scope of this monograph, but consider the following. First is the cost. Second is the potential, depending on the structure, for unintended adverse tax treatment. For example, the "constructive ownership" rules might apply if the arrangement gives the investor almost exactly the same return (and risk) as the underlying investment. In this case, the IRS will recast the transaction as if it were owned directly and will assess nondeductible penalty interest on any underpayment of tax. Third is the difficult question of whether a given index accurately captures the performance of the asset class. The question pertains to issues of survivorship bias, representativeness (bias) in the managers included, stale pricing, and so on.

Another pragmatic issue that arises with a synthetic fund of funds is the fee expansion caused by the asymmetrical performance fees. Hedge fund managers typically get "1 + 20" (that is, a 1 percent fee plus 20 percent of the profits). Consider the result with two managers, each of whom is half of a fund of funds. Manager A makes 40 percent, whereas Manager B loses 40 percent. Because of the performance fees paid to Manager A, the net fee is a hefty 5 percent [that is, $0.01 + (0.4 \times 0.2 \times 0.5)$].

■ *Noninvestment assets.* As noted previously, many expenditures are not consumption, nor are they investments in the sense of having as the primary purpose maximizing risk-adjusted investment returns. Examples of noninvestment assets include homes, vacation homes, yachts, antiques, and works of art.

---

[12]A particular problem with the intermediary's management fee is that it is typically paid on total committed capital but the investor's money is deployed slowly and is outstanding for only a portion of the time the fees are paid. Consequently, the management fee as a percentage of average invested capital can be substantially higher than the stated fee rate.

Certain other types of assets may have investment characteristics but are not structured or intended solely to maximize risk-adjusted return. For example, insurance implicitly has investment characteristics, but its primary purpose is to protect against a major liability or to provide contingency protection rather than to increase wealth. Life insurance proceeds are generally exempt from tax, but that characteristic does not necessarily make them good investments, although many people seem to use insurance as a form of forced saving. Certain types of insurance products create tax-advantaged investment "wrappers," but at a cost.[13] These products have characteristics of both tax shelters and noninvestment assets.

Employment skills also represent an important asset for most people; salary is often the largest single component of their current income. In any financial planning, the investor needs to take into account the entire package of assets, liquid and nonliquid, pure investment and noninvestment. This approach is also true for offsetting gains and losses with complex rules that affect the particular tax treatment.

Summary

The key points to check in evaluating the investment needs of the HNW investor are as follows:
- Ascertain the major components of expenditure liability and categorize them from necessity to highly discretionary.
- Ascertain how much in the way of expenditures is required and, of that amount, how much is consumption and how much is nonconsumption spending.
- Ascertain the investment horizon, not of the investor alone but also of the others who may rely on or succeed in the ownership of the investment assets (e.g., family members, charities).
- Consider the entire family wealth picture in terms of the (current and long-term) intentions of the investor and the opportunity to locate assets in the most optimal way among family members.
- Consider charitable intentions carefully in terms of the high value for tax deferral.
- Carefully consider the interplay between taxation and inflation as they affect net investment returns relating to maintaining long-term purchasing power.
- Finally, when making allocations among asset classes, take into account fees and costs, taxes, inflation, and consumption—not simply optimization of gross returns.

---

[13] A wrapper is a contract an insurance company provides in which the insurer maintains the principal and accumulated interest on an underlying portfolio at book value and guarantees the rate to be credited to current fund investors until the next rate reset. The costs include brokerage fees and commissions, various taxes, high asset management fees, policy fees, and an embedded actuarial-derived profit for the insurance company. One of the authors (Horvitz), in reviewing policies from five large insurance companies, found that only about half of the available tax savings from the most cost-effective (high-dollar, negotiated) insurance products was actually passed on to the policyholder, net of all costs.

5. Overview of Federal Taxation of Investments

U.S. taxable investors must be acutely aware of the federal tax code, which is mind numbing in its complexity. It carries many traps for the unwary but also opportunities to improve after-tax investment performance. This chapter attempts to give an overview of relevant major elements of U.S. taxation; the tens of thousands of pages of tax code, regulations, and rulings and the many court cases interpreting those statutory provisions make adequate coverage of everything impossible. Other countries have tax laws that differ in material ways from those of the United States, but to the extent that elements of those tax laws have similar structures (e.g., taxing income differently from capital gains, taxing only realized gains), much of the investment-related analytical framework in this chapter is applicable, with minor modifications, to other countries.

Because each individual investor's circumstances are likely to result in particular, if not unique, tax issues, and because those circumstances may vary from year to year, investors should seek tax advice that is specific to their circumstances rather than relying on these general principles. The experienced tax practitioner reading this overview will undoubtedly find many arcane exceptions to the general concepts and principles, but for most situations taxable investors will encounter, this simplified framework of taxation can help guide investment choices.

The reader should keep the following points in mind:

1. What most people think of as a tax rate is largely an idiosyncratic function of the investor's mix of types of incomes and deductions and the dollar amount of each; therefore, the investor's effective rate is only somewhat related to the published tax rates.

2. Many investments have return components that receive different tax treatments, which makes it difficult to generalize accurately about the tax efficiency of asset classes.

3. The income tax is only one tax that investors need to be aware of; in particular, the estate tax can be a critical factor in evaluating investment strategies. Other relevant taxes include the alternative minimum tax (AMT), state and local taxes, and foreign taxes.

4. The constantly changing tax laws are a source of significant risk and uncertainty.

The Mechanism of Income Taxation

The federal tax code applied to investments is primarily a profit-sharing mechanism that usually requires payment on investment returns that are actually (or, in some cases, "constructively"—that is, deemed for tax purposes as if actually) received. An important exception to this principle is the tax treatment of certain derivative instruments. For example, U.S. IRC (Internal Revenue Code) Section 1256 contracts are taxed as 60 percent long-term capital gains and 40 percent short-term capital gains when sold or deemed to have been sold (and marked-to-market) on the last day of the calendar year.[14] Another example is the estate tax, which is based on the fair market value of assets irrespective of the amount of unrealized profit.

Understanding that tax is a profit-sharing mechanism is an important insight for understanding the relationship of tax to investments, in that it is not much different from any private profit-sharing arrangement. Effectively, the government "owns" a certain share of the profits from investments, but the government cannot control the timing of the disposition of the investments or when it will receive its share. Unlike the taxpayer, the government has no capital at risk, although its profits will vary proportionately with the investor's. The mechanism of federal taxation is nearly identical to the typical "carried interest" of a general partner in a private equity or venture capital fund except for who controls the timing of tax realizations.[15]

Income, such as interest or dividends, is usually shared between the government and the investor when it is received. Profits on appreciated securities are usually taxed upon sale. Some dispositions or transfers, such as gifts or contributions to a joint venture, may not be taxed at the time of transfer, but the tax is simply deferred. Usually, publicly traded securities cannot be exchanged for other similar securities without paying taxes as if the securities were sold, but certain kinds of private investments can be exchanged for other "like kind" investments and the tax is deferred (see IRC Section 1031). The rules for tax-free exchanges or other dispositions are complex.

Quantifying the amount of tax involves three factors. First is the *tax rate*—the factor that most people think of when it comes to taxation. For most high-net-worth investors the tax rate is the highest marginal tax rate, although lower rates are applied on a sliding scale to taxpayers with low-to-moderate taxable income in any particular calendar year. Because the tax rates and other statutory values in the tax code may become out of date (as they are subject to legislative change), the maximum applicable rates and other statutory numbers *as of the time this book was written* are shown in braces, { }. The reader is cautioned not to assume that the numbers in braces will be in effect in the future.

---

[14] Section 1256 contracts are regulated futures contracts, foreign currency contracts, nonequity (listed) options, dealer equity options, and dealer securities futures contracts. Straddles have special rules. The IRC can be found at www.fourmilab.ch/ustax/ustax.html.

[15] For a more complete mathematical explanation, see Horvitz and Wilcox (2003).

The second factor is the *character* of income to be taxed. Usually, the nature of the underlying investment and the holding period determine the character of the income for tax purposes. Character includes capital gained (both long term and short term), tax-exempt income (which may be exempt from federal and/or state taxes), profits from collectibles, and recapture of depreciation or amortization from investments such as real estate or oil and gas. The investor must pay close attention to the character of income, which determines which rates and which rules about offset apply. Many, if not most, investments have components of taxable income and profits consisting of more than one character. For example, bonds may be taxable both as to interest payments (ordinary income) and price appreciation (capital gains) if sold before maturity.

The third factor is the set of complex rules for *netting* of gains and losses or netting of income and expenses or deductions, which results in the amount to which the tax rate is applied. Netting is functionally the way taxable income is defined and, in many ways, is more significant than the rate itself. The net income calculation entails complex adjustments to gross income involving allowable deductions, exemptions, limitations on deductions and exemptions, application of the formidable AMT, and rules involving the order of offsetting income of different character.

The interplay of these three factors—rate, character, and netting—with the complex rules governing each of them, make it challenging to calculate tax on investments, to estimate and plan in each calendar year, and to maximize after-tax investment return by minimizing taxes. A particularly difficult step is to optimally structure a long-term investment portfolio about which one has much certainty as to the year-by-year tax treatment.

The highest stated rate for federal income tax purposes is {35 percent} for ordinary income, but it is not the maximum effective rate, which is higher. Two main features of the current tax system create this quirk and illustrate the problem of defining "income." The limitation on itemized deductions and on the personal exemption has the effect of making the tax rate higher.[16] The reason is that above the applicable threshold, every dollar of additional income entails a partial reduction in deductions.[17] Deductions are a reduction of taxable income that is first subject

---

[16]The limitation on itemized deductions is scheduled to be rapidly phased out beginning in 2006, but the phase-out itself is currently subject to automatic repeal under a sunset provision in 2011. Normal itemized deductions include state and local taxes or, alternatively, sales tax; mortgage and interest (subject to various other limits); charitable contributions (subject to a maximum of {50 percent} of adjusted gross income, AGI); medical expenses (in excess of {7.5 percent} of AGI); casualty and theft losses in excess of {10 percent} of AGI; job and miscellaneous expenses, usually in excess of {2 percent} of AGI. AGI is defined by IRC Section 62 and generally consists of all taxable income—wages, interest, capital gains, retirement account distributions, and so on—subject to certain adjustments but before deductions and personal exemptions.

[17]Currently, subject to the phase-out, the limit is the lesser of {3 percent} of income above the threshold or {80 percent} of itemized deductions.

to limits based on the specific type of deduction; then, whatever is left over is limited to the excess above a threshold determined as a percentage of the income, which itself must be in excess of a dollar-amount threshold. Effectively, deductions can be "wasted" as income goes up; the effective marginal rate of earning the next dollar is high if it causes the loss of existing deductions.

Alternative Minimum Tax

Related to the problem in limiting deductions is the AMT. Essentially, it is a parallel calculation in which various deductions, exclusions, and credits that would have reduced adjusted gross income (AGI) are added back to calculate a new taxable amount subject to a rate of {0 percent, 26 percent, or 28 percent} depending on the dollar level of income of the taxpayer. For many wealthy investors, the {28 percent} rate is likely to apply. The details of calculating the AMT are too lengthy to deal with here, but one point to keep in mind is that for taxpayers with significant amounts of long-term capital gains and/or tax-exempt income but small amounts of ordinary income, the effect of the AMT is to diminish the tax benefits of long-term capital gains or tax-exempt income. The reason is that any deductions that are already available will be mostly wasted by having inadequate taxable income against which they can be used.

The tax rules are in a nearly constant state of change. Rate, character, and netting are subject to frequent legislative changes (and new interpretations) by both the Internal Revenue Service and the U.S. Tax Court. On complex matters of taxation, the IRS is continually issuing regulations, private letter rulings, technical advice memoranda, and so on, many of which are issued years after the underlying tax rule became effective—and sometimes even after the rule has been replaced. Congress tinkers with tax rates so frequently that history is barely a guide to even the upper and lower ranges of possible tax rates. The political risk of changes, favorable and unfavorable, in tax law is an overlooked aspect of risk management for taxable investors.[18] The high risk of change in the tax law creates an actual volatility of after-tax returns (usually affecting approximately yearly time horizons) that is rarely taken into account by investors as a source, not unlike market volatility, of quantifiable risk.

Treatment of Losses

The IRS has specific, complex rules about the treatment of capital losses on investments. The character of the income usually, but not always, determines the ordering of the application of losses, whereas the principles of netting quantify the net taxable amount.

---

[18]We are indebted to Richard Dahab for this important insight.

The approach in the tax law generally is to require losses to first offset gains of the same character; remaining net losses are used to offset gains of different character. For example, short-term capital losses must first offset short-term gains; then, any unused losses are applied against any net long-term gains (long-term gains less any long-term losses); and finally, any remaining losses can be used to offset up to {$3,000} of ordinary income. Any remaining losses after this can be carried forward to the next year but must be used in the same sequence. Generally, net losses can be carried forward without a time limitation, but they cannot be carried back to adjust taxable income in prior years and cannot be deferred (to avoid using up net short-term losses against net long-term gain, for example). Losses carried forward usually must be used to offset gains in the current year, even if those gains would have been taxed at a lower rate than the rate applicable to the previous losses.[19]

Short-term capital gains are pernicious, in that gains are taxed at the same rate as ordinary income but if the portfolio has excess short-term capital *losses*, they must first be used to offset *long-term* capital gains, which produces an effective waste of tax loss because the long-term capital gains would otherwise be taxed at a much lower rate than the short-term capital gains.

Investment interest expense can be used to offset only investment income, not professional fees and salaries, portfolio income, or dividends. Although excess (net of investment income) investment interest expense cannot be deducted, it can be carried forward to be used in future years. Because the rates for net capital gains and dividends are lower than ordinary income tax rates, capital gains and dividends are not normally used to offset investment interest, although the taxpayer can make an election to do so. Investment interest cannot be used to offset tax-exempt income from municipal bonds. Usually investment losses from passive investment activities (those in which the taxpayer is not actively involved) can be used to offset income or gains only from other passive investment activities.

Special loss limitations known as "wash sale" rules are particularly important for most investors. If an investor sells a security at a loss, that loss may not be recognized if the investor purchases the same or a substantially identical security 30 days before or 30 days after the day of the trade. Although this problem has no perfect solution, commonly used methods to mitigate the restriction include doubling up on shares, waiting the 30 days to repurchase identical shares, and buying shares of a different issuer with similar characteristics (this can also include selling mutual fund shares and replacing them with the shares of a functionally similar mutual fund).

---

[19]For example, collectibles are taxed at {28 percent}. If the taxpayer has a net loss from collectibles carried forward to the next year and then has a long-term capital gain at the {15 percent} rate, the collectible loss carryforward must be used to offset long-term capital gains, thus "wasting" part of the tax value of the prior-year loss. Long-term capital losses, however, which otherwise are worth only {15 percent}, can be used to offset gains from collectibles at the {28 percent} rate.

Tax Treatment of Different Asset Classes

Different asset classes are subject to different types of tax treatment and are affected differently by all three of the quantifying factors—rate, character, and netting. The following subsections provide examples of the general tax treatment of certain asset classes.

Fixed Income. The tax treatment of bonds should be simple, but it is not. Generally, the return from fixed-income securities comes in the form of price changes (appreciation or loss) and interest income. The majority of bonds pay interest, which is taxed at ordinary income rates, but many variations can be found among bonds, each of which has its own special tax characteristics. Most bonds create long-term capital gains (or losses) or short-term capital gains (or losses) if sold before maturity. Some of the more common types of bonds are briefly described here:

- Zero-coupon bonds create annual tax liabilities for imputed but unpaid interest.
- U.S. Treasury instruments are taxable for federal purposes but not taxable for state income tax purposes.
- U.S. Saving Bonds (Series EE/E, HH/H, and I) are exempt from state and local taxes, and federal tax is deferred.
- Government agency bonds are taxable at the state and federal level.
- Municipal bonds are generally tax exempt at the federal level but are exempt from state income tax only if the bonds were issued in the same state in which the investor resides. Certain types of private-purpose municipal bonds are functionally taxable at the federal level because they may cause the taxpayer to be subject to the AMT {26 percent or 28 percent}. Bonds sold at a premium or discount to the adjusted purchase price will incur capital gains or losses.
- Mortgage-backed bonds (and other asset-backed bonds) usually pay a mixture of taxable interest and untaxed principal amortization.
- U.S. (and certain non-U.S.) corporate bonds create ordinary income as to the interest component.[20]
- Non-U.S. bonds, corporate or sovereign, are generally taxed the same as corporate bonds.
- Interest from Treasury Inflation-Indexed Securities (commonly called TIPS) is taxed as ordinary income, but TIPS are also taxed currently as ordinary income for the inflation-related adjustments to the principal value. The gross adjustment to principal directly changes the cost basis, dollar for dollar.

---

[20]When evaluating bonds and dividend payments from corporations, the investor should consider that, although bond interest is taxable to the investor, it is deductible to the corporation whereas dividends are paid from the corporation's after-tax earnings. When corporate and individual tax rates are similar, the net effect in terms of combined taxation is about a wash for interest payments but not for dividends. So, interest becomes the more tax efficient, even for taxable investors, when substituted for what would otherwise be a dividend-paying equity.

- Bonds purchased at a premium or discount to face value have a variety of tax treatments, some optional and some not. Also, the treatment of amortized premiums and discounts may depend on the type of bond or how it was purchased or sold. Here are some of the main types:
    1. bond with original issue discount or premium,
    2. municipal bond,
    3. government bond issued before 1982,
    4. bond with original maturity less than one year,
    5. bond with a market discount (sold for less than face value), and
    6. bond with a market premium (sold for more than face value).[21]

Clearly, the investor's after-tax return from fixed-income investments is more complicated than simply the nominal rate of return of the bond; it is a function of the character of the income (which may be derived from one or more return components of the bond), the netting (e.g., application of the AMT), and the applicable tax rate for each component. A particular investment portfolio that has attractive after-tax returns in one calendar year may be more or less attractive in subsequent calendar years depending on the particularities of the investor's tax position as it relates to other items of income, loss in the future, and changes in the three tax factors.

Stocks. Stocks generate returns from dividends and from price changes. Dividends used to be taxed as ordinary income (for most high-net-worth investors, at the highest marginal rate), but tax changes have reduced the tax to the same rate as the rate on long-term capital gains {15 percent}, subject to the complex restrictions to prevent trading simply for tax benefits of the wash sale rules.[22] The current wash sale rules are (1) for common stock, the investor must have held the stock for more than 60 days during the 120-day period beginning 60 days before the ex-dividend date and (2) for preferred stock, the investor must have held it for 90 days during the 180-day period beginning 90 days before the ex-dividend date. Note that a put or in-the-money call restarts the holding period, which must be tested each record date.

Capital gains and losses for stocks depend importantly on the holding period. Short-term capital gains rates (historically, the same as ordinary income rates) apply to securities held for 12 months or less. Long-term capital gains rates, at {15 percent}, are significantly lower than short-term rates, at {35 percent}. Thus, capital gains can be taxed much more favorably (i.e., long term) for as little as a one-day difference in holding period. During the last quarter of the 20th century, long-term rates went

---

[21]The rules for amortizing *discounts* and *premiums* for municipal bonds are different from the rules for taxable bonds.

[22]The long-term capital gains rate for low-income taxpayers is only {5 percent}.

back and forth between 20 percent and 28 percent. For a brief time, the law included an 18 percent rate for securities held five years or more. Such changes are evidence of the instability, and hence volatility risk, of the tax component of net returns.

Accurate and detailed record keeping is critical to identifying the specific tax lots to be sold so as to maximize long-term capital gains and minimize short-term capital gains. If investors do not have adequate records to identify the specific tax lot of stock sold, they must use the "first-in, first-out" method. Average cost for allocating the tax basis across different security lots can be used for most mutual fund shares.

Mutual Funds and Exchange Traded Funds. Mutual funds are a type of pass-through entity. With minor exceptions, net capital gains and dividends from the securities held by a mutual fund are distributed each year to the fund's shareholders. In addition to intentional turnover that creates capital gains, or merger and acquisition activity that creates involuntary capital gains within a fund, large redemptions by shareholders can create liquidations of securities that result in involuntary capital gains. At the end of the year, those investors remaining in the fund will have to pay taxes on their pro rata share of the capital gains, even if they did not redeem any shares themselves. For mutual funds that have embedded net gains, new investors must also recognize these gains as distributed or at year-end. This recognition can create unexpected tax problems. Losses cannot be taken by the taxpayer unless fund shares are sold; however, they are netted against gains within the mutual fund. Investors who use dividend reinvestment plans and who have sold shares at a loss may be subject to wash sale rules if the sales were not carefully timed. For large investors, some mutual funds will make in-kind distributions; this approach saves on transaction costs, but for tax purposes, in-kind distributions will be deemed sales and will be taxable.

Exchange traded funds (ETFs) are publicly traded securities that usually hold a basket of stocks, such as an index, but can also be actively managed. The tax treatment is a cross between treatment of a single stock and treatment of a mutual fund. Because of the way ETFs are structured and traded, the market price is close to the net asset value, and when shares are sold, the investor recognizes a capital gain or loss. Turnover within the funds and dividends or interest are taxable to the shareholders. Unlike mutual funds, however, the redemptions by other shareholders do not create tax recognition for the remaining investors. As a result, ETFs can defer capital gains distributions more efficiently than mutual funds—a significant advantage.

Neither mutual funds nor ETFs are well suited for tax-loss harvesting controlled by the private investor because the volatility of these portfolios is less than the volatility of the underlying stocks, although the fund manager can use tax-loss harvesting within the fund. The tax lots available for harvesting are only the shares in the fund, not the individual securities held within the funds. Tax-loss harvesting is more effective with separately managed accounts.

Real Estate. Investment real estate profits are taxed in multiple ways: Net rents are treated as ordinary income, long-term capital gains are taxed at a special intermediate rate, and the recapture of previously taken depreciation expense is taxed at a third rate (IRC Section 1250). Real estate (or mortgages) held by a real estate investment trust (REIT) is generally treated in a manner similar to the treatment of a mutual fund. The tax characteristics of the underlying investments are carried through to the shareholder; that is, no tax is paid by the REIT, which must distribute substantially all its income annually. Real estate partnerships, like all partnerships, are pass-through entities that pay no tax themselves, but tax is paid by the partners, generally in proportion to their partnership interests, and the original character of the income is unchanged. Although tax-free exchanges can sometimes be accomplished with real estate held by a partnership, directly held real estate is best suited to tax-free exchanges (IRC Section 1031). Personal residences are treated differently from personal vacation homes, and both have tax treatments that are significantly different from the treatment of real estate held for investment purposes.

Collectibles. Profits on collectibles, such as works of art, are subject to either short-term capital gains tax {35 percent} or a special long-term capital gains rate {28 percent}. The netting of gains and losses against other types of capital gains is unfavorable if collectibles are sold at a loss but favorable if they are sold at a gain.

Private Equity and Venture Capital. Private equity and venture capital funds (including funds of funds) are typically limited partnerships that are treated as pass-through entities; the tax characteristics of the underlying investments are carried through to the investor (i.e., no tax is paid at the partnership level). The management fees charged by investment partners may sometimes be deductible as an expense against ordinary income, whereas the net gains are usually long-term capital gains because of the longer holding periods of the underlying illiquid investments.[23]

Hedge Funds. Hedge funds are also treated as pass-through entities; most hedge fund gains come in the form of short-term capital gains, however, because of the funds' high-velocity trading or use of derivatives (e.g., IRC Section 1256 contracts, which are taxed at a statutory 60 percent long-term rate and 40 percent short-term rate when sold or deemed sold at marked-to-market values at the end of the year). Some hedge funds treat their activities as a business and qualify as "traders." Net income is taxed at the higher ordinary income rates, but the expenses of trading and operations can be deducted against gross trading profits. Traders making an IRC Section 475 election, which requires mark-to-market recognition

---

[23]Some private equity funds have been attempting to recharacterize their management fees so as to get long-term capital gains treatment. Long-term versus short-term treatment makes no difference to the tax-exempt limited partner, of course, but short-term treatment significantly raises the cost to the taxable limited partner. Whether this technique will survive IRS challenges remains to be seen.

of income, can receive even more favorable treatment of expenses and losses. To qualify as traders, some hedge funds may claim aggressive tax status that may not be sustainable if challenged by the IRS. For investors who are not traders, fund expenses are subject to the limitation on deductions of {2 percent} of AGI and interest expenses are a separate itemized deduction.

Before investing with a hedge fund, the prudent investor should thoroughly understand the prospective tax treatment of the fund—for example, by looking at the historical tax returns of the fund and considering IRS challenges to tax positions taken by the fund. Multistrategy funds, particularly so-called global macro funds, are usually more difficult to assess prospectively because the tax character of the underlying investment strategies is likely to vary greatly over time.

Individuals as Businesses or Traders. It is not easy for most individuals to qualify as traders because the IRS takes a strict approach to accepting trader status. To qualify, taxpayers generally need to show that their trading activities are done almost daily and for a livelihood, that the number of trades and dollar amounts are significant, that significant time is spent trading, and that the holding periods are short.

Derivatives. A variety of derivative financial instruments receive special statutory tax treatment. Generally, these instruments are exchange traded options and futures (including IRC Section 1256 contracts) sold by securities dealers in the normal course of their business and traded in the public markets. Most derivatives that typical investors encounter are either taxed at the short-term capital gains rate if sold during the year or taxed as IRC Section 1256 contracts with 60 percent considered long-term capital gains and 40 percent considered short-term capital gains, for a blended effective rate of {23 percent}. Nondealer futures contracts are usually treated as if they had the same character as the underlying investment would have had if held directly by the investor.

Synthetic Hedges and "Constructive Ownership." A wide variety of techniques, with all sorts of variations, are available for attempting either the conversion of ordinary income or short-term capital gains into long-term capital gains or for creating the effect of a sale without the tax consequences. The tax rules are complex and must be analyzed in the context of the specific transaction.

If a security position is so completely hedged that substantially all of the risk is removed, the IRS may recharacterize it as a sale and tax will be due as if it were sold. Guidance on how much the investor must remain at risk to avoid having the transaction deemed a constructive sale is limited.

Derivative contracts can be used in various ways to create more favorable tax treatment than that given the underlying investment. Sometimes, intermediary pass-through entities are created to hold a highly taxed investment; then, investors purchase derivative instruments that have the same or very similar pretax total returns, with the gains of the derivative instrument taxed as long-term capital gains. But when derivatives are used to create such synthetic hedges with nearly identical economics to the underlying investment assets, the IRS tries to ignore the overlay for tax purposes. So, an investor may be deemed to have constructive ownership, which can result in a tax treatment as if the asset underlying the derivative instrument were, in fact, directly owned by the investor. Gain in excess of any underlying long-term capital gains will then be treated as ordinary income, and nondeductible interest will be charged on the underpayment of tax.

Estate and Gift Taxes

The estate tax (or "death tax") follows a different principle and has a different function from income taxation. The estate tax is applied to the fair market value of assets irrespective of whether unrealized gains or losses are involved. Intense debate is going on as this book is being written about either eliminating the estate tax entirely or raising the exemption amount high enough that only the very wealthiest estates will be subject to it. The 2005 estate tax exemption is $1,500,000, and the exemption is scheduled to rise to $3,500,000 by 2009.[24]

Related to the estate tax is the generation skipping transfer (GST) tax. This onerous tax functions as a two-step estate tax and affects estates left to grandchildren, either directly or in trust. Assets left to a grandchild are treated as if left to the decedent's child who then immediately died and left the same assets to his or her child. The estate tax, if any is due, is paid on the estate and then taxed again on the net amount. For example, if the estate tax was 45 percent and an estate was over the exemption by $1 million, the first layer of tax would be $450,000 (leaving $550,000), and the second layer (because of the GST) would be an additional 45 percent of the $550,000.

Related to the estate tax and the GST tax is the gift tax, which is applied to certain transfers during the taxpayer's lifetime. Under current law, each taxpayer is allowed to "gift" *inter vivos* (during life) up to {$11,000} per recipient to an unlimited number of recipients and has a cumulative lifetime exclusion of {$1 million}. Payment of a gift tax can mitigate or even eliminate the application of the estate tax. Previously, the estate and gift amounts excluded from tax were linked as a unified credit, but they no longer are.

Appreciated assets get a step-up in cost basis, so for estates not subject to tax, all *unrealized* gains become permanently tax free. Unrealized losses from assets that have gone down in value are lost permanently, however, except to the extent that

---

[24]Under current law, the estate tax is to be repealed entirely in 2010 but only to be revived in 2011 at $1,000,000, the amount in the previous law. This nonsensical approach is almost certain to be replaced with some new estate tax law before it happens.

an estate subject to tax is that much less valuable. The new tax basis is the fair market value at the time of the heir's death.

For transfers by gift rather than inheritance, the rules about cost basis for gifts other than cash are complex.[25] Appreciated property generally has a tax basis equal to the tax basis in the hands of the transferor. The new tax basis for assets that have decreased in value, however, is the fair market value at the time of transfer. In some instances, unrealized losses are wasted in the gifting of depreciated property. For gifts or inheritances on which estate or gift taxes are paid, the tax is allocated on a pro rata basis between the original tax basis (cost) and the appreciation, to create a new basis in the hands of the transferee. Transfers to a spouse are exempt from any gift tax but retain the adjusted basis of the transferor for tax purposes. Transfers to a spouse can also be made through a qualified terminal interest property (QTIP) trust, which can restrict the spouse's power to appoint the principal but allows the spouse to have lifetime income. Estate tax is due upon the death of the surviving spouse. *A QTIP trust can be very valuable in extending the deferral of unrecognized gains.*

The federal estate tax is perhaps the most important overlooked tax in investment planning and should receive far more attention from investors and their advisors than it currently receives. As onerous as the estate tax is and as complex as the rules involving estate and gift taxes may be, careful planning can often eliminate or substantially mitigate the tax burden, albeit usually at the expense of control during the investor's lifetime.

States also have estate taxes that should not be ignored in investment planning. Historically, the states and federal government essentially shared the estate tax that was collected through a system of tax credits for estate tax payments. Because of recent changes in the federal estate tax, states have been receiving less money and are rapidly moving to amend their estate taxes to make up the difference. Most of these changes will result in a combined federal and state estate tax that is significantly higher than the federal tax alone.

The federal estate tax law provides an opportunity to artificially create and partition the *income* streams from the *remainder* streams that are provided by an asset or investment. The income stream may be based on the actual return (an income trust) or some defined percentage return (a "unitrust"), usually called a "life estate." The remainder interest may be determined when the investor (or others) dies or for a fixed period of years. The variations are numerous; most are known by acronyms [e.g., GRAT (grantor retained annuity trust), GRUT (grantor retained unitrust), GRIT (grantor retained income trust)]. Counterparts give either the income stream or the remainder to a charity for the investor to take a current charitable deduction [e.g., CRUT (charitable retained unitrust), CLAT (charitable

---

[25] IRC Section 1014 is to be replaced by IRC Section 1022 after 2009, in the absence of further legislative changes, which will materially change the ways the step-up and carryover tax basis are treated.

lead annuity trust), CRAT (charitable retained annuity trust)]. These vehicles have potential for arbitraging the tax rates of the components and also for arbitraging the statutory discount rate used to value the transferred component compared with the actual return on the investment. In some respects, these vehicles are the tax equivalent of derivative financial instruments and can be analyzed accordingly.

Tax-Sheltered Saving Accounts

The federal government provides tax incentives for various retirement and other savings accounts. Rather than cover each one in detail, because they are subject to legislative change, an overview of their general characteristics is in order.

Tax-sheltered accounts can be analyzed on the basis of whether the amounts deposited are before or after tax and whether the withdrawal of amounts is taxable or nontaxable. Accounts funded with after-tax money (e.g., Roth individual retirement accounts) can usually be withdrawn tax free, but accounts funded with pretax money [e.g., a regular IRA or 401(k)] are usually taxed at ordinary income rates on the full amount of distributions, both principal and profits, when withdrawn.

In any event, their central feature is that while the money is held in the account, it compounds without current taxation. Only when the current and future tax rates are different does an opportunity arise not only to compound tax free but also to have an arbitrage of the different tax rates. For very wealthy investors, the amount of money that can be put into these accounts may not be significant. For investors willing to use tax-deferred investments, such as tax-managed index funds that are subject to only a {15 percent} tax rate, Roth IRA accounts may not add value, especially if the estate is not likely to be taxed.

Deciding which types of assets should be held in a tax-sheltered account and which should be held outside is complicated and highly conditional on such factors as expected changes in future applicable tax rates. (This topic is discussed more fully in Chapter 9.) Generally, investments that produce mostly current income and/or ordinary income subject to high tax rates should be held in a tax-sheltered account; other assets can be held outside. When considering where to put fixed-income securities, advisors and investors should keep in mind the penalties for early withdrawals from tax-sheltered accounts. Most investors' fixed-income holdings are intended to provide security, and using the money if it is needed may require withdrawals at inopportune times.

State Taxation

With 50 state taxing jurisdictions (plus many local tax jurisdictions), this chapter cannot thoroughly discuss the tax regimes in each.[26] When potential after-tax returns are calculated, state taxes can be used as a deduction against income for federal tax purposes; however, these deductions are subject to important limitations (e.g., the itemized deduction limitation). In quantifying the applicable marginal tax rate for calculating the combined federal and state tax applicable to investment returns, an advisor should take into account the deduction of state tax from federal tax, which is subject to various limitations.[27] In other words, an investor cannot simply add the two tax rates together.

International Taxation

Like the United States, other developed countries usually have some tax on returns from publicly traded companies domiciled in the country. Dividends and interest may be subject to withholding taxes that, in theory, can be recovered, in whole or in part, by U.S. taxpayers if the subject country has a tax treaty with the United States that allows recovery. The paperwork for recovering these withholding taxes can be burdensome. When investors are considering professional investment managers, they should inquire about the ability of the manager to recover non-U.S. withholding taxes. Generally, taxes in other countries that are not recovered can be taken as a credit or deduction against income. Certain non-U.S. jurisdictions are considered tax havens and do not tax foreign nationals' investments domiciled there. The effectiveness of these tax havens is under constant attack by the IRS, however, and their value is questionable for most investors.

Key Tax Questions in Analyzing Investments

The major points of this chapter can be summarized by considering the key questions related to taxes that the investor or investment advisor should ask when analyzing an investment.

First, what is the *character* of the components of expected return:

- ordinary income;
- dividends;
- long-term capital gains;
- short-term capital gains;

---

[26] For example, Florida has no income tax but does have an "intangible" tax levied against the fair market value of publicly traded securities. Massachusetts has an income tax, which historically has differentiated interest and dividends from capital gains. In Massachusetts, rates for interest dividends and earned income have become the same as for long-term capital gains but short-term capital gains and profits from collectibles are taxed at more than double those rates {12 percent versus 5.3 percent}.

[27] As of this writing, one can deduct either state income taxes or state sales taxes but not both.

- asset class–specific tax rates—collectibles, real estate, recaptured depreciation, oil and gas depletion allowances, and so on;
- federal tax exemption;
- state/local tax exemption;
- foreign income subject to withholding?

Second, given the character of the income, the AMT, and the limitation on deductions, what will be the effective marginal tax rate for the nth dollar of return?

Third, what deductions, expenses, or offsets are available to reduce the tax on the investment return? Does this investment make the most efficient use of those potential benefits? Will the taxpayer be subject to the AMT, and if so, how will being subject to the AMT affect the net treatment of taxable income?

Fourth, especially for periods of fewer than 12 months, what is the anticipated holding period of the investment?

Fifth, how will potential future changes in tax rates affect the after-tax risk and return attractiveness of the investment?

Finally, how will the long-term attractiveness of the investment be affected by the application of the estate tax?

6. Techniques for Improving After-Tax Investment Performance

The taxable investor in the United States has many options for improving after-tax return by decreasing the effect of the tax bite. Many investors do not take full advantage of what is available to them by law, however, and their advisors or investment managers do not pay close enough attention to the need to manage toward the lowest effective tax rates. This chapter first presents an overview of the most obvious and relevant techniques for improved after-tax investing by U.S. investors, followed by a summary of some of the less-used techniques. The presentations are not a substitute for specific advice from tax professionals that takes into account the unique circumstances of the investor, and many technical details must be lost in such an overview.

Tax-Lot Management

The first essential step in any tax-aware investment program is adequate record keeping. Although not required by law, keeping the lot-by-lot price, quantity, date, and associated commission costs of investments is in the investor's interest. In selling securities, it allows the investor to identify which specific lot was sold. When multiple purchases are made of the same security, each purchase has an associated cost or tax basis. By identifying the specific lot(s) for disposition, the investor can minimize current recognition of gains by picking those tax lots with the least associated tax liability. If the records are not adequate and each trade cannot be properly identified with a specific tax lot, an investor is required to use first-in, first-out accounting, with the earliest-acquired lot's tax basis used first. For mutual funds held by a broker or institutional custodian, the investor may use the average cost basis, but this approach is not as tax effective as specific lot accounting. The U.S. Internal Revenue Service (IRS) does, however, let the investor direct a broker or mutual fund (in writing) to always deliver for sale the highest-cost-basis stock first without making the specific identification at the time of each trade.

Holding 12 Months for Long-Term Capital Gains

Nothing adds value to the private investor's portfolio so simply and effectively as holding securities for at least 12 months to qualify for long-term capital gains treatment. At current U.S. tax rates of {35 percent} for ordinary income and short-term capital gains versus {15 percent} for long-term capital gains, literally 20 percent (35 percent − 15 percent) of all profits are at stake in the holding-period decision.[28] In other words, the investor keeps 85 percent of the profits after paying long-term capital gains tax but only 65 percent of the profits after paying tax as ordinary income or short-term capital gains. To make up such a difference, an investor would need a rate of return 31 percent higher for the same investment—all for merely changing the holding period. An 8.0 percent return subject to long-term capital gains tax is equivalent to about a 10.5 percent pretax return subject to ordinary income tax or short-term capital gains rates. State and local taxes can make this difference even greater.

Unlike recognizing short-term gains, selling a security at a short-term *loss* in less than 12 months provides no disadvantage. Because short-term capital losses must first be used to offset short-term capital gains, however, then offset long-term capital gains, and only at this point offset (a limited amount of) ordinary income, the effective rate at which the losses are used is dependent on the nature of the other gains.

Table 6.1 provides a simple example of the powerful effect of the holding-period differences on terminal wealth. Such differences make it hard to justify short-term trading for the ordinary taxable investor. Those who believe that they can successfully overcome the tax disadvantage by phenomenal results may wish to seek qualification as a business (or "trader") for the purpose of trading securities, at least so that expenses, which otherwise cannot be deducted, can offset profits that will be treated as ordinary income.

Table 6.1. Additional Wealth from $10,000 Invested after Different Return and Tax Rates Applied

Return and Tax	5 Years	10 Years	20 Years
Rate of return = 5%			
15% LTCG tax	$2,310	$ 5,160	$12,990
35% STCG tax	1,730	3,770	8,960
Rate of return = 10%			
15% LTCG tax	$5,040	$12,610	$41,120
35% STCG tax	3,700	8,770	25,240

Notes: LTCG = long-term capital gains; STCG = short-term capital gains.

---

[28]Recall that tax rates and other statutory values in the tax code are shown in braces, { }.

Investment managers who reach a negative view about a security they have purchased within 12 months may be concerned that the client will complain if the stock goes down but the manager has held it in order to get long-term capital gains treatment. A clear understanding with the client from the beginning as to the tax benefits that are certain with near-term stock price changes but are highly uncertain with a stock sale may mitigate this dilemma for the manager.

For investors who anticipate a short-term holding period (e.g., have a near-term strong bullish or bearish market sentiment), the tax burden can sometimes be mitigated by using futures contracts or listed options. For example, rather than buying the S&P 500 Index itself for fewer than 12 months, the investor can buy the futures contract, which will be taxed at a statutory rate of {60 percent} long-term capital gains and {40 percent} short-term capital gains for a blended rate of {23 percent}, which is less than the short-term capital gains rate of {35 percent}. A further explanation of tax choices for investment horizons of less than one year, one to five years, and more than five years is given in Gordon and Rosen (2001).

Tax-Loss Harvesting

Tax-loss harvesting is the voluntary sale of a security at a loss for the express purpose of currently recognizing the loss for tax purposes. In most circumstances, taking such losses is in anticipation of using them to offset gains in the same tax year, but sometimes, it may be worthwhile to warehouse losses that can be carried forward into future tax years, especially if those losses are expected to evaporate in the future. One of the key problems with taking current losses solely for tax purposes is the difficulty of replacing the sold security immediately. The "wash sale" rules (although more detailed than given here) generally require that the same, similar, or functionally equivalent security cannot be purchased 30 days before or after the sale if the loss is to be recognized for tax purposes (see also Chapter 5).

A loss taken now saves taxes if, and only if, the investor has offsetting taxable gains. Special rules require that losses offset gains in a particular order, even if high-tax-rate short-term capital losses wind up offsetting low-tax-rate long-term capital gains. Unused losses can be carried forward indefinitely into the future. To the extent that losses can be used to offset gains and save taxes, more net-of-tax money is available for repurchasing the same or substitute securities, but when a repurchased or substitute security is sold in the future, the difference will result in a recapture of the loss (subject to certain exceptions to be discussed).

Whether current recognition of capital losses is used to offset current gains elsewhere in the portfolio or losses are "banked" as tax-loss carryforwards to be used against future gains, many investors do not understand that taxes saved now by taking losses are usually simply postponed. Although net losses may be carried forward to use in future years, taking the loss provides no utility if the investor has no prospects of other gains for offset, now or in the future. In other words, losses are not valuable in their own right. When a tax loss is taken and a substitute security is purchased at a lower cost, a new tax cost basis is established at the lower cost. The result is the possibility for an even larger gain that may have to be recognized in the future.

A simple example will clarify what happens. Suppose an investor purchases stock in Company XYZ for $100 and a year later, it is trading at $80. The investor sells it for a loss of $20, which offsets some other long-term capital gains the investor received. At a long-term capital gains rate of 15 percent, the investor would save $3 in taxes that would otherwise have had to be paid. With $80 of sales proceeds plus $3 of tax savings, the investor could reinvest a total of $83 in another security (or wait 30 days and buy XYZ again); the $83 would become the new cost basis for tax purposes. The investor would have additional purchasing ability of 3.75 percent ($3 ÷ $80) because of the tax savings, so (at the $80 market price) she could buy 3.75 percent more shares of XYZ than she had before. But the new tax basis of $83.00 is $17.00 less than the original basis of $100.00. If the repurchased securities appreciate, any new gain will include the $17.00 reduction in basis that came about as part of the tax-loss harvesting.

If the investor never sells the substitute stock and her estate is not subject to estate tax, either because the estate is less than the amount of the estate tax exemption or because the estate is going to charity, the government never recaptures the tax savings from the loss. The government also may not recapture it from investors who are subject to the estate tax because the estate tax is based on the gross fair market value irrespective of the amount of unrealized gain. In the example, the investor's estate on which taxes will be due (if taxes *are* due) may become somewhat larger because the investor may be able to advantageously reinvest the tax savings from the tax-loss harvesting; in this case, the government partially recoups the earlier tax savings.

Arnott, Berkin, and Ye (2001) simulated tax-loss harvesting by using S&P 500 stocks and a 35 percent tax rate. They found:

> A great deal of loss harvesting is possible in the first few years; the earnings on the associated tax savings lead to an immediate and dramatic increase in relative portfolio value. After the first five years or so, the pace of gain added begins to diminish rather sharply. Yet, even after 25 years, the tax alpha is *still* adding about 0.5% per year to portfolio wealth, an alpha that most active managers can't add reliably pre-tax, let alone after tax. (pp. 13–14)

When they took deferred taxes into account, they found "a much more moderate early benefit, but it quickly compounds and builds over time" (p. 14). Even after 25 years, the tax alpha was still almost 50 basis points a year. At the 2005 lower tax rates, this tax alpha would be lower but would not be erased. When a 20 percent tax rate was used, the authors still found a median increase in terminal wealth of 8 percent after 25 years.

Using a similar methodology but with 2003 tax rates and various stock indexes, Stein (2004b) found essentially similar results—with postliquidation tax alphas averaging around 40 basis points a year in Year 10 to Year 30. As expected, the particular simulation results were affected by tax rates, length of holding period, market return, and volatility.

But tax-loss harvesting should not be taken lightly or done too frequently. Done incorrectly and without regard for the recapture and the transaction costs of selling and rebuying, the unwary investor can experience undetectable losses that result in a slow hemorrhage of wealth. No tests or measures will directly show the effect, but it will surely erode value. On balance, it is better to err on the side of conservatism by forgoing some possible current tax savings so as not to incur transaction costs that might ultimately prove to be more than the present value of the tax saved from harvesting. That is not to say that tax-loss harvesting should be restricted to year-end actions. Gordon and Rosen discussed timing and suggested techniques for mitigating the effect of the wash sale rules that otherwise prohibit taking losses if the same (or essentially the same) security is purchased 30 days before or after the trade date. These techniques include

- doubling up on shares,
- doubling up forward conversion, and
- writing out-of-the-money puts.

A rigorous analytic procedure for determining the absolute optimum strategy for tax-loss harvesting is not yet available for practical use, but choosing policies that clearly add value is not difficult. For example, a constraint that must be satisfied is that the net present value of tax deferral exceed the round-trip transaction cost of selling and buying a replacement security. The calculation of this breakeven threshold is more subtle than it sounds, however, because the net tax savings depend on the likelihood of increased consequent taxes at a later point in time. This likelihood depends, in turn, on such myriad factors as average turnover rate, life expectancy, and whether an estate tax will be due.

If one always realizes a loss when the net benefit is only slightly above zero, the cumulative effect on terminal wealth will be only slightly above zero. Consequently, a better policy is to wait until the loss is larger. Determining how much larger analytically requires determining when to exercise a complicated tax option. Monte Carlo simulation allows one to try out various tax-loss harvesting strategies, however, to see how the strategies would perform in a range of market conditions and assumed future tax-paying contexts. The strategies can be made contingent on the size of the individual loss, the volatility of the stock, its return correlations with the market as a whole, the presence or absence of loss carryforwards, and so on.

Tax Deferral and Turnover

The effect of minimizing turnover was well documented by Jeffrey and Arnott (1993). Their focus was on turnover as a proxy for average gain recognition; that is, average turnover of 20 percent implies that, on average, approximately 1/5 of the portfolio has gain or loss recognition in any given year. Obviously, not all turnover creates realized gains, because some turnover generates taxable losses; nonetheless, with the stock market having a long-term positive rate of return, turnover is generally a bad thing with respect to taxation—except for the option of tax-loss harvesting. Jeffrey and Arnott noted that the benefits of low turnover are nonlinear—not material unless very low turnover rates are reached.

Stein (2004a) likened tax deferral to an interest-free loan from the government. Although, superficially, this view is plausible, the source of value from tax deferral is actually something else. The fundamental issue is not the time value of money but, rather, participation in profits. The government is a silent risk-sharing partner in the investing but one that puts up no capital. The sharing mechanism is nearly identical to the carried interest in a private equity or venture capital partnership. The government has a claim on a share of all current income recognized, which includes interest and dividends, but the share of a capital gain is usually due only upon realization of the gain, the timing of which is mostly at the option of the investor. The way tax deferral adds value is through the differential compounding at a pretax rate of return versus at an after-tax rate of return. The longer the compounding goes untaxed, the greater the terminal wealth, subject to the single-period negative return of the final tax payment at the time of liquidation.[29] Jeffrey and Arnott suggested that the term "interest-free loan" as applied to tax deferral is unfortunate because it incorrectly implies that any future taxes are already assets of the Treasury and are simply due at the borrower's option.

For most investors and in most normal market conditions, somewhere in the vicinity of 10 years are needed to accumulate sufficient tax alpha from the differential in the compounding rates to make tax deferral an important factor for after-tax wealth. This finding is contrary to the assertions of those who believe relatively short-term tax deferral to be worthwhile. For holding periods longer than 8–12 years, the improvement in after-tax results starts to become material, and for very long holding periods, the potential for an enhanced effective after-tax rate of return is quite significant—on a par with the manager alpha alleged by many successful active managers.

The power of long-term tax deferral is shown in **Table 6.2**, which compares returns for various holding periods for a tax-exempt investor, an investor deferring all capital gains recognition until final liquidations, and an investor who pays long-term capital gains tax on all gains annually.

---

[29]The mathematics of tax deferral is fully described by Horvitz and Wilcox.

Table 6.2. Wealth Accumulation for Investors with Various Strategies
($1,000 invested at 6% steady rate of return)

Years to Liquidation	No Tax	Tax Deferred	Annual Tax
5	$1,338.23	$1,287.49	$1,282.37
10	1,790.85	1,672.22	1,644.47
15	2,396.56	2,187.07	2,108.83
20	3,207.14	2,876.07	2,704.30
25	4,291.87	3,798.09	3,467.91
30	5,743.49	5,031.97	4,447.15

Tax Deferral and the Estate Tax

For investors with long investment horizons, estate tax treatment can enhance the value of tax deferral. The estate tax is applied to the fair market value of assets held at death irrespective of the amount of unrealized profit. Even at the highest estate tax rates, voluntarily realizing capital gains during one's lifetime is never better than holding the estate unless an increase in future tax rates occurs and the unrecognized gain will not pass through one's estate untaxed. Consider the following:

- For investors for whom little or no estate tax will apply, the entire unrealized gain will completely escape taxation forever, and a step-up in cost basis to the fair market value at time of death will occur for the heirs.
- Investors who leave their estates to charity can avoid the estate tax.
- Assets above the exemption amount can be left to one's spouse without paying estate taxes, although no step-up in basis occurs and taxes may be due (above the spousal exemption amount) when the spouse dies.

As deferral times lengthen or the deferral puts the liquidation into the posture of an untaxed estate, the effective rate of return approaches the return for a tax-exempt investor.

In summary, tax deferral is valuable for investments that will be included in the investor's estate, is otherwise not important for U.S. individual investors other than for long holding periods, and can add value for long-term investors comparable to the alpha from successful active management.

Tax-Advantaged Savings and Retirement Accounts

Various forms of tax-deferred savings and retirement accounts add value in much the same way as the tax deferral described in the previous section, but a potential complication is that the tax rate on money coming out of these accounts may not be the same rate that would have applied at the time of the contribution.[30]

---

[30]Tax-deferred accounts are discussed also in Chapter 5.

For very wealthy individuals, various offshore vehicles also allow the tax-free compounding of gains indefinitely. Upon repatriation of the profits, however, all the profits will be taxed as ordinary income. A {5 percent} nondeductible interest charge is also applied to the foreign income on which tax was not paid (to adjust for the time value of the deferred tax payments). Certain elections avoid the penalty but effectively negate the off-shore deferral advantage. For tax purposes, some states do not follow the federal rules but tax only profits earned in the calendar year of repatriation.

Certain types of offshore vehicles require special elections if income is not to be imputed as annual taxable income.[31]

Municipal Bonds

If markets were in perfect equilibrium and all taxable investors had the same tax rate, municipal bonds would trade with a yield correctly adjusted for their tax-exempt status; in other words, the advantages would be arbitraged away. But municipal bonds are not always priced to be equivalent to an instrument with equal credit, equal duration, and taxable yield; the difference is as much a factor of the investor's tax situation as of the market. The trading costs and the bid–ask spread for municipal bonds can greatly exceed those for comparable taxable bonds, and this factor should not be ignored. Particularly at the short end of the market, municipal bonds may sometimes be unattractive in yield if corporations in higher tax brackets are competing with individuals for yield.

Because municipal bonds are also exempt from state and local taxes if the issuer and the investor are of the same state, the breakeven yield has to take into account the net effect of state taxes, adjusted for their deduction against federal income. This analysis is not straightforward because of the various deduction limitations and the alternative minimum tax (AMT).

When the tax-exempt municipal bond yields are compared with the yields of U.S. Treasury securities (which are exempt from state and local taxes), the municipal bond advantage may be less than when the municipal bonds are compared with other taxable fixed-income instruments. For high-bracket investors taxable at the {35 percent} rate from the states with the highest income tax (e.g., California at {9.3 percent}), taxable yields may need to be as much as 1.7 times the tax-exempt yield to make the taxable bond worthwhile. Moreover, certain private-purpose bonds are seemingly tax exempt but are subject to the AMT, which creates a high effective marginal tax rate.

The fundamental question, then, is whether the tax-exempt yield is more or less than the taxable yield for an *equivalent* security. For this comparison, equivalency must take into account a number of factors in addition to yield, including

---

[31]See the rules for passive foreign income corporations at www.irs.org.

- the tax character of the accreted market discount,[32]
- transaction costs (which are higher for municipal bonds),
- liquidity (which is potentially lower for municipal bonds),
- mispricing (mispricing of the bonds and the bid–ask spread is more common in the municipal market),
- early redemption provisions (which allow issuers of municipal bonds to call, or prepay, the bond).

When the investor needs to trade bonds prior to maturity—for example, for portfolio rebalancing—these factors can become particularly important. Before advisors recommend that taxable investors buy *only* municipal bonds, advisors should also give proper consideration to the benefits of taxable bonds.

Alternative Minimum Tax

The AMT creates a quagmire of problems and issues for the taxable investor.[33] Although the taxable investor is generally better off with long-term capital gains at their lower tax rate than short-term gains, some degree of taxation from ordinary income may be desirable because of potential AMT issues. That is, if the investor is likely to be subject to the AMT, it may be wise to look for investments that produce high nominal returns subject to a higher tax rate because the effective marginal tax rate may make the net returns more attractive. Because of the complexity of the AMT, the advisor may need to model various investment scenarios to determine the likely optimal mix of ordinary income, short-term capital gains, and long-term capital gains. AMT rates are {26 percent} for up to {$175,000} of AMT-defined income and {28 percent} for greater income.

Capitalizing the Income Stream

Stocks have two components of return—price change and dividends. Bonds also have two components of return—price change and interest. For taxable bonds, the interest is ordinary income, generally taxed at a {35 percent} rate, whereas price appreciation, other than the accreted discount, is taxed at long-term capital gains rates if the bond is held longer than 12 months.

---

[32] Recall that when a bond is purchased in the secondary market, the difference between the purchase price and its stated redemption price at maturity is the market discount; the accreted (or accumulated) market discount is treated as ordinary interest income in the year the bond is sold, redeemed, or transferred. For tax-exempt bonds, the effective yield may be a blend of taxable and tax-exempt income and, therefore, may be less after tax than the same effective yield from a tax-exempt bond purchased at par.

[33] See also Chapter 5.

When interest rates have declined since the purchase of a bond, the investor may sometimes be able to improve after-tax investment returns by selling the appreciated bond, paying the capital gains tax on the sale, and reinvesting the net proceeds in a greater number of bonds bearing a lower coupon rate. This tactic is known as "capitalizing the income stream." The strategy presumes that the investor faces a capital gains tax rate that is lower than the tax rate applying to coupon interest (as is true in the United States for holding periods exceeding 12 months). In general, because the price changes of bonds that occur solely in response to interest rate changes adequately reflect pretax fair net present value, the unrealized capital appreciation is a close approximation to the pretax present value of the future income stream.[34] This strategy would not apply to holdings in tax-exempt bonds because an investor would not want to trade tax-exempt income for a capital gains tax liability. In practice, trading costs make this kind of bond-tax swapping most useful with very liquid bonds.

Portfolio Tilts

When dividend rates were higher than capital gains rates, some commentators argued that portfolios with low dividend yields were preferable for taxable investors. Stocks with low dividend yields may be growth stocks and efficiently using earnings for growth (capital appreciation) instead of paying out dividends. Much of the historic literature on the return from growth stocks versus the return from value stocks indicates that over long periods of time, value stocks outperform growth stocks. Whether this pattern continues or not, although portfolio tilts do change the risk and return characteristics of portfolios, with long-term capital gains rates identical to dividend tax rates, neither high nor low dividends offer any obvious advantage.

Tax Sheltering with Swaps and Other Derivatives

Tax-shelter swaps are another method of attempting to convert ordinary income to long-term capital gains. Swaps generally involve taking some difficult-to-quantify risk because of unclear and changing legal interpretations.

Changes in the "constructive ownership" rules eliminated the benefits of many types of swap transactions previously in use. Wall Street has nonetheless creatively developed other swap products in an attempt to get around the constructive ownership problem. The general form of these swaps involves some sort of counter-party (and thus some counterparty risk). The most common version is a total-return swap, in which the investor deposits money with a counterparty, who then invests in various investment funds, securities, or other assets. The counterparty agrees to pay an amount to the investor equal to the future value of the total return minus the costs of the swap and its administration.

---

[34]Because the wash sale rules do not apply here, an investor can immediately repurchase the same security.

To be successful, these swaps must adhere carefully to certain tax rules and must be considered with expert tax advice. Also, these tax swaps are unlikely to last a decade;[35] so, the tax-deferral component is not likely to be of much value, although the conversion of ordinary income to long-term capital gain, if successful, is valuable. The various legal issues involved with tax swaps are far beyond the scope of this book, but to the extent that the swaps pass legal muster, they add value primarily by converting what might be ordinary income or short-term capital gains into long-term capital gains. Certain types of transactions—for example, call options on hedge fund returns—give the investor the choice of taking losses as ordinary income or gains as long-term capital gains.

Insurance Wrappers

Investments held in a variable universal life insurance policy are particularly well tax advantaged. A sum of money is paid to the insurance company, up front or over a period of years, out of which life insurance premiums are paid and the balance is invested. The insured person need not be the same person as the owner, which creates the potential for transferring wealth without any transfer tax (gift or estate tax) because death benefits are tax free. Customized insurance products for large amounts have the advantages of lower negotiated fees and some flexibility and customization of the underlying investments.

Insurance products have been used to shelter (if held until death) or defer (if redeemed) returns from investments. Typically, payment is the cash surrender value if the policy is terminated before death or the greater of cash surrender value or death benefit if the policy pays off at the death of the insured person.

Analyzing the value of insurance is complicated. To take advantage of the tax-sheltering characteristics granted to the insurance industry, the investor must be willing to pay a number of fees and costs:

- mortality charges (the cost of the insurance protection based on actuarial projections),
- federal and state taxes on premiums,
- administrative charges,
- sales loads, and
- investment management fees.

Mortality charges are usually embedded in the whole life product but should be approximately equivalent to the term insurance costs of an equivalent death benefit. The expected return for most investors will be slightly negative, as would be anticipated because the insurance companies are in the business of making money from term insurance. The other costs are usually straightforward. Investment

---

[35] Wall Street firms are generally reluctant to create structured products for longer than five years.

management fees are typically market rates or somewhat higher. Taken together, these fees are a significant drag on nominal returns and represent a significant hurdle to adding value or improving after-tax returns.[36]

Tax Asymmetries and Hedging

A topic too little explored in finance literature is the challenge for taxable investors of using derivatives to hedge. A simplified example will illustrate the types of problems that often go unrecognized. Suppose a dollar-based U.S. investor is purchasing $1,000 of an exchange traded fund (ETF) holding euro-denominated European stocks. The investor wants to hedge the euro currency exposure, and he uses $1,000 of euro futures to hedge the currency. Consider two possible scenarios:

1. In less than 12 months, the exchange rates change, causing the value of the ETF to go down $100 (from currency) and the value of the futures to go up $100. The futures have a short-term capital gain of $100, and the ETF has a short-term capital loss of $100—an exact offset. The investor is appropriately hedged on an after-tax basis.

2. In more than 12 months, the same thing happens, but now, the tax treatment is different. The futures are U.S. Internal Revenue Code Section 1256 contracts taxed at the end of each calendar year as marked-to-market sales with a rate of 60 percent long-term and 40 percent short-term gain/loss for a blended rate of {23 percent}. The ETF gain/loss is taxed as a long-term capital gain/loss at a {15 percent} rate. The investor liquidates both positions and has an $85 after-tax currency loss from the ETF but only $73 of after-tax profit from the futures. When large dollar amounts are involved, such a mismatch has a serious effect.

Complex hedging and swapping arrangements have to take into account tax treatment, as well as the more conventional factors, to ensure appropriate after-tax matching.

Portfolio Rebalancing

Portfolio rebalancing is an admirable goal, but it is not without cost, including tax consequences. The taxable investor needs to be cognizant of at least two important issues that do not affect tax-exempt investors.

First, the tax on unrecognized gains in the portfolio is effectively "owned" by the government, so in determining when an asset class is outside its target range, the *net* (of tax liability), not the gross, amount is the correct value to use in the

---

[36]In an unpublished analysis, Horvitz found that large privately negotiated variable life policies were generally not worthwhile without a lengthy holding period. The breakeven point was at the 8-year to 12-year mark—similar to the point at which tax deferral becomes material. Roughly half of the tax benefits (under 2005 and higher tax rates) were retained by the insurance companies in the form of fees and costs, and the other half accrued to the benefit of the policyholder.

calculation. Therefore, rebalancing will usually be somewhat less necessary or need to occur less often for taxable investors than they may realize. This factor is especially important in rebalancing multiple asset classes with different proportions of unrealized gain.

Second, the cost of rebalancing requires taking into account the loss of tax-deferral benefits as well as direct transaction costs. For short or medium time periods (e.g., less than about 10 years), the value of any tax deferral is not likely to be meaningful, but for longer periods, it can be significant. The analysis of rebalancing should account for the trade-off between the benefits of deferral and the benefits of risk–return management. (An example is given in the Appendix B.) The use of derivatives in rebalancing is fraught with the same issues mentioned in previous sections. A somewhat more detailed discussion of these issues is in Horvitz (2002).

Summary

Investment tax strategies fall into a few broad categories:

- Convert the character of taxable return from high-tax ordinary income or short-term capital gains into low-tax long-term capital gains.
- Delay the recognition of gain or income for long periods of time.
- Hold off the recognition of gain or income until death so that only the estate tax, if any, applies.
- Create voluntary losses to offset current gains.
- Use government-sanctioned tax-sheltering vehicles (e.g., retirement accounts or insurance wrappers) to defer or eliminate taxation of investment returns.

Even when these various strategies have superficial appeal, however, the investor should be cautious to analyze the costs involved and should carefully weigh cost against the possible savings. Tax savings that may be only temporary may not be worth the up-front costs.

Although general rules of thumb are a good starting point (for example, municipal bonds are suitable for taxable investors), a complete understanding must include a detailed analysis of the investor's specific tax circumstances—now and *in the future*. This analysis must take into account *income and deductions from all sources* and an estimate of the *final disposition* of the investment assets. Investment advisors should also recognize that the tax rates and rules are constantly changing, so savings that depend on no changes in the status quo of the current tax rules may evaporate unpredictably in the future. Stein (2004a) provides an analysis of the impact of future tax increases.

Part III
Organizing Management
for Private Clients

This part of the book concerns the needs of the professional money management organization as it tries to organize to best serve HNW clients. Even family offices focused on the needs of a single family may find the ideas helpful as the number of family members and interrelated but legally separate portfolios increases. Chapter 7 revisits many of the issues noted in previous chapters but from the specific viewpoint of the managing organization. It goes on to address organizationally useful procedures for eliciting investor goals and preferences and for measuring performance. Chapter 8 deals with the "manufacturing" approaches needed to deal with large numbers of HNW accounts while still providing effective customization.

7. Institutional Money Management and the High-Net-Worth Investor

The common practices of investment management professionals who normally deal with large tax-exempt institutions require considerable change to be effective in dealing with a clientele of high-net-worth (HNW) individuals. For institutional investment firms, the key ingredient to success is the ability to understand and forecast the behavior of investment assets. In short, this kind of management is all about the markets. For investment professionals serving HNW clients, the complexity and heterogeneity of individuals require that efficient adaptations to the needs and preferences of specific investors be the centerpiece to which the bulk of intellectual effort and resources is devoted. This chapter explores recommended practices for serving an HNW investor. In doing so, the chapter reviews certain basic investment concepts and briefly notes numerous complex issues that are more fully developed elsewhere in this book.

Identifying the Private Investor's Objectives

The proper goal of the investment management process, whether for an institutional investor or an HNW individual, should be to produce investment results that best fulfill the investor's objectives. In the terminology of economics, the goal is to maximize the *utility* of the investor.

Three basic concepts of investor utility introduced by the mathematician Bernoulli in 1738 are still the basis of most methodologies in money management. The first concept is that investors prefer to earn more return on their investments rather than less. The second is that investors prefer less risk to more risk, although they may have difficulty describing exactly what risk is. The third is that investors exhibit decreasing marginal utility of wealth; that is, if someone is wealthy enough to own four different houses, gaining the wealth to buy house number five is less important than gaining the wealth to buy the first house. The sort of vast wealth increases that might allow an individual to fund extreme luxuries (e.g., buying a private island) are unlikely to arise from conventional investment portfolios, except over very long time horizons; so, such increases are usually given minimal attention in formulating investment policies.

A numerical way of conveniently expressing Bernoulli's ideas is to say that the investor's goal is to maximize the logarithm of his or her wealth. Levy and Markowitz (1979) showed that the log of wealth function can be closely approximated by a simple function of the mean and variance of periodic returns. Investor goals can be summarized as trying to maximize risk-adjusted returns—that is, the arithmetic average of the expected returns minus a penalty for the risk (i.e., variance of returns) that must be incurred to obtain the returns. The size of the risk penalty can be scaled to reflect the aggressiveness of the investor.

Refinements of Mean–Variance Optimization. A common criticism of the Markowitz approach is that it deals with only the mean and variance of return and does not consider higher moments, such as skewness or kurtosis. Cremers, Kritzman, and Page (2003) showed, however, that, with a few notable exceptions, the mean–variance method is fully sufficient to accurately express a wide range of utility functions for the purpose of allocating assets within an investor's portfolio.

Defining exactly what "risk-adjusted" means is not trivial in a practical context. If one makes the assumptions that the investor's only goal is to maximize expected wealth *in the distant future* and that the investor has all the information necessary to form the exact distribution for the expectations, then a risk adjustment that maximizes expected geometric mean return is appropriate. In the real world, however, investors care about what happens *in the interval* between now and the distant future and they must base their expectations only on their forecasts of an unknown future, not on exact foreknowledge about the distribution of future events. In other words, they not only don't know the future return, but they also don't actually know the probability distribution of future returns. Contrast this situation to roulette, where the players don't know which number will come up next, but they know exactly the odds of the game. Therefore, investors are, sensibly, more risk averse than required to merely maximize the geometric mean return.

An approach to describing investor behavior more usefully than simple frameworks for investor utility is Wilcox's concept of "discretionary" wealth (described in Chapter 2). In this concept, investors seek to maximize the geometric mean return on the portion of their wealth they can afford to lose without unacceptable consequences. This mathematical construct can be used to define the right level of risk aversion to be applied in calculating risk-adjusted returns for the portfolio as a whole.

Finally, in extending this theoretical concept of risk-adjusted returns to the real world, keep in mind that investing is rarely costless. It entails fees to be paid to investment managers, transaction costs, and often taxes on the realized profits. The advisor can include these ideas in the framework by describing investor goals as trying to maximize *risk-adjusted returns, net of costs*.

The Individual's Utility Function. The process of describing the utility function of most institutional investors is relatively simple: For most pension funds, endowments, and insurance companies, the magnitude and timing of spending can usually be forecasted with reasonable precision. The goal is to maximize the risk-adjusted returns, net of costs, for the institutional investor's portfolio while maintaining sufficient liquid assets in the portfolio to fund the fulfillment of liabilities in a timely fashion.

The ultimate goal for most investors is to not merely accumulate wealth but to accumulate wealth so as to provide for the funding of consumption at a later date. In the case of individuals, the need to fund consumption during the person's own lifetime may be modest relative to the available wealth, so consumption is deferred to future generations or charitable organizations who receive bequests. Both the high uncertainty of demand for consumption by descendants and the lack of actuarially sufficient sample sizes make investment policy formation for wealthy individuals far more difficult than it is for institutional investors. The money management professional must respond to the potentially conflicting needs of the HNW investor with a great deal of planning and care. In addition, individuals may face tax liabilities that are large in magnitude and arcane in computation.

Consider a case in which an HNW client hires an investment manager with the instruction that a particular investment portfolio not generate more than $1 million in net capital gains during the upcoming tax year. The investment manager must research the likely impact of this constraint on investment success and inform the client if meaningfully better returns, and thus more wealth, could be obtained within a less restrictive constraint on gain recognition.

Unlike most institutions, individuals have finite lives. Their family circumstances and lifestyles evolve through time. These changes call for constant adjustment in the balance between returns obtained and risks taken. Unlike large institutional investors, which routinely employ actuaries and consultants to help form appropriate financial policies, many wealthy, even very wealthy, individuals have minimal professional advice in this regard. The investment management firm must thus assume the responsibility of educating their investment clients about appropriate financial policies.

The situation for HNW investors can be further complicated in a number of common ways. Individuals and families generally want to fund consumption (e.g., a new car) that is less predictable than the spending of typical institutions. Often, the investing goals of individuals are intertwined with the saving and consumption goals of other members of their families. Few wealthy families struggle with the dual need to save for retirement while funding expensive educations for their children. Finally, the HNW investor may have a variety of personal preferences that are entirely unrelated to financial matters. For example, individuals who are concerned about the environment or other important societal issues may direct that their investments be arranged in what they perceive to be a socially responsible fashion so as to avoid providing implicit financial support to companies or governments whose behavior they find objectionable.

With careful thought, most of the complexities associated with investing for HNW individuals can still be expressed through the basic concept of risk-adjusted return, net of costs. If conflicts among the various goals and preferences of the investor become too great, however, expressing the conflicting goals in tractable algebraic terms becomes difficult. In such cases, the investment professional must exercise judgment based on detailed communication with the investor. Ensuring consistency of qualitative policies can be difficult, however, for a large set of heterogeneous clients and in differing market conditions. Retail brokers are generally governed by regulations similar to the New York Stock Exchange's "know your customer" rule that requires brokers to have at least a specific set of facts about their clients' financial circumstances and investing experience. This information is often captured in a standardized questionnaire that can serve as the starting point for assessing the investor's financial needs. Bolster, Janjigian, and Trahan (1995) suggested procedures for converting an investor's answers to such questionnaires into explicit portfolio weights for asset allocation by using a technique called the "analytic hierarchy process." Related work by Detzler and Saraoglu (2002) extended the approach into mutual fund selection.

Taking Taxation into Account

Taxation of investments made by HNW individuals is quite different even from the taxation of institutions that do pay taxes on their portfolio gains, such as insurance companies, nuclear decommissioning trusts (in the United States), or pension funds in some countries (e.g., Australia). Taxes on investments generally occur at three points (at least) during an individual investor's lifetime.[37] First, taxes are sometimes due immediately on the income arising from an investment, such as bond interest or dividends from stocks. Second, the rise in value of investments may be subject to a capital gains tax when that investment is sold, irrespective of whether the proceeds will be used for consumption or reinvested in another asset. Third, the returns to tax-deferred vehicles, such as retirement plans [e.g., 401(k) plans in the United States], allow investments in the plans to realize income and capital gain without immediate taxation, but taxes are levied when the funds are withdrawn from the plan.[38] The tax includes both the accumulated investment profits and any original investment capital that was not taxed at the time it was originally earned. To the extent that an investor's portfolio would be subject to additional taxation from any of these sources if it were liquidated, the investor has a *contingent tax liability*.

---

[37]See also Part II.

[38]Keep in mind that the income used to make the investment in the first place is itself (in most cases) after-tax money.

A fourth point at which taxation may occur is upon the death of the investor. Many countries have some form of "death tax" based on the value of the estate that is passed upon death from one individual to heirs. The size of the estate, the nature of the assets, the need for liquidity, and the tax circumstances of the investor's portfolio during her or his lifetime—all can affect the magnitude of estate taxes. Depending on the individual's estate tax expectations, the investment policies likely to prove most beneficial for that particular investor can vary substantially. In addition, at the time this book is being written, some jurisdictions (such as the United States) are considering changing (minimizing or eliminating) estate taxes. Thus, the element of uncertainty surrounding the estate tax should also be incorporated when formulating expectations about estate taxes for a particular investor.

When Doing Well for the Client Appears Bad for Business

An obvious consideration for taxable investors is that *how much return your investments earn matters less than how much investment return you get to keep.* This important issue can easily get lost in the context of the relationship between an investor and a hired investment management provider. The disconnect arises because, to attract clients, the investment management firm has to demonstrate the effectiveness of its services. To the extent that HNW investors all come with investor-specific circumstances involving taxes, preexisting investment positions, and a variety of constraints and to the extent that the investment manager handles the account in accord with these circumstances, the performance of any one investment account can be judged only in its own context. That performance record is not helpful in demonstrating the manager's skill to others. In addition, the heterogeneity of taxable clients will naturally cause dispersion in the returns achieved by different investors. Although this dispersion can be affirmative evidence that an investment manager is actually doing a good job of customizing to each client's needs, many in the investment industry presume that the dispersion arises from poor quality control of the investment process across the many accounts managed by the firm. Therefore, many investment managers continue to focus their attention on obtaining pretax returns in excess of their benchmarks, even if this goal is not desirable for the investor.

Deferral of taxes is almost always a positive contributor to investor wealth. Consider a hypothetical investor in a 50 percent tax bracket. If that investor invests at 10 percent for 20 years on a tax-free basis, he will accumulate $6.73 for every $1 originally invested. If the investor earns the 10 percent gross return but pays taxes annually, the return falls to 5 percent after taxes and the accumulated wealth is only $2.65 for each $1 originally invested. If the investor earns 10 percent for 20 years but defers the payment of taxes to the end of the period, the taxes on the cumulative profit will be $2.86, leaving the investor with terminal wealth of $3.87, the equivalent of a 7 percent a year after-tax return.

The dramatic impact of taxes on investment returns has been amply demonstrated in the financial literature. Dickson and Shoven (1993) and Dickson, Shoven, and Sialm (2000) showed that performance rankings of mutual funds on a pretax and after-tax basis are nearly unrelated. KPMG (see Wolfson 2000) has distributed an extensive white paper detailing the dramatic effects of taxation on mutual fund investors.

Performance Measurement of Taxable Portfolios

Since 16 April 2001, the U.S. Security and Exchange Commission (SEC) has required that all public mutual funds that accept capital from taxable investors report after-tax returns for 1, 5, and 10 calendar years in their advertisements (see SEC 2001). Two forms of the after-tax computation are required. The first assumes that the investor still holds his or her fund shares but has paid taxes due on any income or capital gain distributions during the measurement period. The second method assumes that the fund shares were sold at the end of the measurement period. Obviously, the tax rates assumed in these illustrative calculations may not be applicable to a specific investor.

The measure of gross investment returns is relevant to decision making only in the case of an investment that is truly tax free. For taxable or tax-deferred investments, appropriate estimates of after-tax rates of return should be used in making decisions about the attractiveness of particular investments or portfolios. In broad terms, forecasts of after-tax investment returns can be formulated in two ways. One approach formulates expected after-tax returns as a function of pretax returns and, given some anticipated level of portfolio turnover, the expected level of taxes. A more complex approach adjusts expected returns for taxes on the forecasted level of investment income (dividends and interest) but explicitly treats capital gains taxes as a form of expected transaction cost to be levied upon liquidation of each specific investment security.

Both the optimal asset allocation and the appropriate balance between active and passive strategies can be dramatically altered by the consideration of taxation. Many active strategies that appear attractive on a pretax basis do not offer the expectation of any after-tax excess returns.

An important issue in the relationship between professional money managers and their investor clients is how to judge the performance of the funds in comparison with appropriate benchmarks. Through both the Global Investment Performance Standards (GIPS®) and its predecessor version, the AIMR Performance Presentation Standards (AIMR-PPS®),[39] CFA Institute requires that "after-tax" return calculations be based on either the "anticipated tax rates" or the maximum federal

---

[39] Effective 1 January 2006, AIMR-PPS standards will converge with GIPS standards and the AIMR-PPS standards will be dissolved.

(or federal/state/local/city) tax rate or rates applicable to each client.[40] It also requires that if any taxable accounts are included for the purposes of composite performance reporting, all taxable accounts managed according to a similar investment objective or style must be included. When such after-tax returns are compared with pretax returns for popular benchmark indices, the managed accounts obviously look like they are underperforming.

The simple answer is to create after-tax benchmark indices. As discussed in Stein (1998), however, such a task is much more complex than it seems. A benchmark could, seemingly, simply measure the taxes arising from a hypothetical index fund based on the particular index in question and then compute the after-tax return. The cost basis of the index fund would depend on when shares were purchased, however, and at what prices. Therefore, the after-tax return of the index fund for a given period would depend on the starting date of the index fund. The after-tax return for 1999 for a fund started in 1990 would be different from the performance of funds started in 1985 or 1995 because the cost basis of the positions would be different. Gulko (1998) proposed a time-weighting scheme to deal with this issue. In addition, cash inflows and outflows paralleling those of the investment account for which comparison is desired must be included in the simulation of the index fund for most precise comparison.

The most recent guidance published under the GIPS standards goes further than the earlier standards in addressing the matter of after-tax performance measurement. The current standards still require that realized taxes be included in return measurement simply as a cost. The standards now recommend that, in addition, the contingent tax liability (i.e., the taxes that would be payable if the investment account were liquidated immediately) be reported to investors as collateral information when investment returns are reported. Note that the use of the word "contingent" in this context does not imply optional; it is being used in a fashion consistent with accounting terminology. The liability is contingent (rather than absolute) because if the investments are held to a later date, they may fall in value to an extent that no gain has been made and, hence, no payment of taxes is due. Investors can thereby assess whether the contingent liability has grown or fallen during the reporting period and consider the implications for their wealth. Discussion continues as to whether a scheme similar to that adopted for mutual funds by the SEC should be incorporated into the CFA Institute standards.[41]

An important related issue is that of the contingent tax liability associated with purchasing public mutual funds in the United States. If an investor buys into a fund that has a preexisting liability for capital gains taxes, the investor may be taxed on fund profits that were actually received by other investors during prior time periods.

---

[40]CFA Institute was formerly the Association for Investment Management and Research.
[41]See www.cfainstitute.org/cfacentre/ips/pdf/Taxation_Provisions.pdf.

These taxes are then reflected as an adjustment to the cost basis of the mutual fund investment, so the situation really represents an acceleration of tax payments rather than an overpayment.

Concentrated Portfolios

HNW investors may have portfolios concentrated in a few holdings rather than in many diversified holdings. Frequently, such concentrated portfolios arise because of the belief that the realization of capital gains on a portfolio position with a low cost basis will create such a large tax liability that it outweighs the benefit of lower risk through portfolio diversification.

To the contrary, diversifying portfolios is often in the interest of investors, even if it means incurring significant taxes. A detailed mathematical analysis of the risk–tax trade-off is provided in Stein, Siegel, Narasimhan, and Appeadu (2000). They analyzed the problem by transforming it into a "tax-deferred equivalent" basis. The optimal decision is taken to maximize the net present value of the trade-off between paying taxes (reducing asset value today) and better diversification (lower risk, better long-term compounding).[42]

Relative and Absolute Return

Because explicitly defining investor goals and preferences is difficult, judging the performance of an investment manager in terms of whether the (often vaguely defined) goals have been achieved is difficult. Therefore, it has become customary in the investment industry to judge the performance of a manager on the basis of performance relative to a benchmark market index or a peer group of other managers rather than performance in meeting predefined objectives unique to the client. But consider a situation in which an investment manager achieved a return of −10 percent in a period when the benchmark index had a return of −15 percent. Is the manager a hero for outperforming the benchmark by 5 percentage points or a fool for having lost 10 percent of the investor's money? The answer may be either or both, depending on the investor's relative concerns about absolute return and risk in relation to benchmark-relative return and risk.

Almost all investors have two parallel concerns about the returns from their portfolios. They are concerned about the *absolute* returns from the portfolio and also about how the returns on the portfolio compare with the returns earned by other investors, proxied by the market.[43]

---

[42] See also the example in Appendix B.

[43] In aggregate, the average returns of other investors can be presumed to approximate the return on broad market indices because for someone to be above average in return, someone else must be below average in return.

Institutional investors often put more emphasis on *relative* rather than absolute return and risk. For example, a corporate pension fund will be concerned that it have sufficiently good returns to meet its liabilities to pension beneficiaries, but it will also be concerned that the returns earned be competitive with the returns earned by the pension funds of companies against which the sponsoring company competes. If the pension fund earns less return than those of competing companies, the pension-related expenses of the sponsoring company will be greater, placing the company at a competitive disadvantage. Because of taxes, HNW investors tend to be more concerned with absolute return and risk. Taxes are generally levied on profits made from absolute investment returns, not market-relative returns. Note that taxes in most countries are levied on individual security transactions, not at the asset-class level. Therefore, the effect of taxation on the investor's preference for absolute risk and return cannot be adequately addressed through a change in asset allocation policy. Suppose an investor's portfolio is divided between a stock portfolio and a bond portfolio. Even if the asset allocation inputs are changed to reflect the expected after-tax returns and the after-tax volatilities of the two asset classes, the change will not reflect that the cross-sectional dispersion of returns in each portfolio is larger for a stock portfolio than for a bond portfolio. Therefore, the stock portfolio offers greater opportunity for tax-loss harvesting and may be somewhat more attractive (and worthy of greater allocation) than even an after-tax asset allocation would suggest.

The formulation of investment policy that simultaneously considers both the absolute and the market-relative context has been studied by Chow (1995). He found that the concept of "risk-adjusted returns, net of costs" still holds. Because investment returns add linearly, an increase in absolute return for an investment implies an equal increase in the market-relative return for the same period. The concept of risk-adjusted return needs to be extended, however, to include two separate penalties for risk—one for absolute risk and another for benchmark-relative risk. The risk-aversion scalars used in the two penalties will take on different values that convey the investor's relative concern about the two sources of risk. With two separate risk penalties, the familiar concept of the efficient frontier along two dimensions (return and risk) becomes a three-dimensional surface (return, absolute risk, and relative risk).

Luckily, one can frame the problem as having only two terms—return and risk—relative to a specially constructed benchmark. One can think of absolute risk as risk around a market index consisting of only cash. The portfolio can then be managed to a single benchmark that is a combination of the selected market index and cash. If an investor has twice as much concern about absolute risk as she has for relative risk, she could have a joint benchmark consisting of one-third the regular benchmark index and two-thirds cash. Once the investor and investment manager have agreed on such a joint benchmark, the manager's performance can be properly judged with respect to the investor's simultaneous concerns for both absolute and relative risk. HNW investors with sufficient wealth that the primary purpose of investing is to accumulate additional wealth for bequest to future generations do emphasize market-relative returns as a proxy for long-term purchasing power.

Investment policies are routinely formulated to express concerns about inflation, but some investors' needs to hedge inflation may be even greater than usually understood. The cause is the "wealth effect," as studied by Mehra (2001) and other economists, wherein individuals increase their discretionary spending as they feel wealthier.

Finally, it should be noted that tax payments truncate the distribution of absolute return outcomes. By sharing in an investor's profits, the government also shares in the risk to the extent that losses can be used to offset gains on other investments. Thus, the absolute risk tolerance of taxed investors should be higher than it is for otherwise comparable tax-exempt investors.

The wealth of private investors may also take the legal form of a trust, in which the income of capital and the growth of capital are payable to different beneficiaries. This characteristic may further complicate asset allocation by requiring some level of minimum income.

Summary

HNW investors, with needs that are both complex and far more heterogeneous than typical institutions, represent a great challenge to the investment professional. In an institutional investment process, the vast majority of intellectual effort is dedicated to forming advantageous expectations about the future return distributions of financial assets. Relatively little effort is expended on adapting the investment process to the needs and preferences of specific investors. Effective investment management for the HNW individual requires that the area of relative emphasis be reversed, giving precedence to the intelligent adaptation of the investment process to the needs of the individual.

Minimization of taxes must be considered a crucial element of performance together with pretax return and risk. What matters is not how much return investors make but how much they get to keep.

Absolute returns may be of equal or greater importance than market-relative returns for the HNW investor.

Convincing clients of what is really in their best interests (and thereby attracting and retaining clients) may not be easy. Therefore, as a business, investment management for HNW investors has particular challenges.

8. Portfolio Management as a Manufacturing Process

The heterogeneity of high-net-worth (HNW) investors poses a special challenge to investment professionals. A large investment services firm may have thousands, even tens of thousands, of clients. The challenge of providing investment services that are simultaneously highly customized to the needs of individual investors and also having the research depth and analytical rigor commonly provided to institutional investor clients may seem insurmountable. This chapter describes a strengthening industry trend of bringing the operational disciplines of a "portfolio manufacturing" process into investment management practices. The chapter also provides a review of common practices in investment firms serving an HNW clientele.

"Mass Customization" of Portfolio Management

The clear goal of portfolio manufacturing is to allow mass customization of investment services but with a high degree of quality control. This approach is not greatly different from the efficient operation of industrial concerns, such as the auto industry, that have mass-produced goods to individual customer order for many years. In most traditionally organized investment services firms, the same individual investment officer may be responsible for maintaining the relationship with the investor client, participating in the firm's investment research process enough to reflect the firm's investment views in the client's portfolio, and maintaining routine supervision of the client's portfolio.

In the portfolio manufacturing paradigm, the investment process is separated into three distinct roles:

- maintaining client relationships to understand the needs and wants of the investor (like a car dealer),
- investment research and overall portfolio management (like auto engineers), and
- customizing the investment products offered by the firm to the specific needs of the individual client (running the factory floor to fill individual client orders).

As noted in Chapter 2, the bulk of customization for HNW clients involves tax issues, but many other factors can demand modifications of investment strategies.

The typical setup of the "assembly line" in portfolio manufacturing consists of a core of automated functions for analyzing each investor's portfolio on a regular and frequent basis (perhaps daily) and proposing transactions believed to be optimal in the current circumstances. The analyses are then reviewed by portfolio management personnel and approved or not. Every investor's portfolio is provided regular attention in a process of uniformly high quality. In the automation process, the core functions must be connected to the investment firm's accounting system so as to provide the managers with information about investor portfolios and a database of the investor preferences and constraints, and it must be connected to the firm's trading functions so that approved transactions can be implemented.

Investment accounts belonging to HNW investors are particularly labor intensive. Each account is different. Each has different tax circumstances arising from the different cost bases of investment securities held and the particular tax rates and regulations in the investor's state or country of domicile. In addition, investment accounts are commonly transferred to a new investment management firm in the form of preexisting positions, rather than as cash (the customary form of transfer with institutional investors). Finally, each account may be part of a group of accounts that, in aggregate, are the investment assets of a family or another interrelated group of individuals.

In a typical bank trust department, each investment officer oversees 200–300 individual accounts. According to a report from the consulting firm Cerulli Associates, some investment firms believe that with an automation platform, they can achieve productivity of up to 1,500 accounts per investment professional. Firms following the manufacturing approach have, essentially, completely automated many routine portfolio management functions (e.g., withdrawing cash from an account in a tax-sensitive fashion). Their investment professionals can thus spend their time on the subtle aspects of investment analysis and portfolio management that rightly require human judgment. Correctly implemented, the manufacturing approach improves investing results and saves money for the investment firm because it allows the most expensive resource, investment professionals, to be used in the most efficient fashion.

For the wealthiest investors, investment services have traditionally been highly customized. Their particular needs and preferences have been catered to by trust companies, specialized consultants, and family offices. Unfortunately, because of the complexities in the situations of HNW investors, many researchers have assumed that complicated investment methods cannot be applied to this group of investors. Therefore, the development of sophisticated investment methods applicable to HNW investors has lagged behind the rest of the investment industry. Only since about 2000 has a significant amount of rigorous research emerged on issues relating to HNW investors.

For investors with less investment capital than HNW investors, the opportunities for customization have been slim. Investment brokerage firms commonly offer "separately managed account" (SMA) programs to individual investors with sizable investment funds, but these programs provide no customization; rather, in these programs, investors own a legally separate copy of a model portfolio formulated by an external investment manager. Such an account does remove the conflict of interests inherent in a brokerage account for an individual investor.[44] SMAs may also allow large individual investors to diversify across several managers. Some programs, however, offer less customization for accounts under $100,000.

Unfortunately, SMA arrangements provide few benefits to investors not provided by a portfolio of mutual funds. Additionally, investment firms that offer no customization may run the risk that the U.S. Securities and Exchange Commission will view a large number of identical accounts as an unregistered (and hence illegal) mutual fund. Nevertheless, SMA programs are growing rapidly in popularity. In 2003, Cerulli Associates predicted that SMA assets in the United States will reach $2.6 trillion by 2008. Through the portfolio manufacturing approach, several investment firms have succeeded in bringing a high degree of customization to the SMA market.

Tax Management for the HNW Market

Taxation is of great importance to individual investors. Many active management strategies do not offer even the expectation of after-tax excess returns, as demonstrated by Jeffrey and Arnott (1993). Dickson and Shoven (1993) found little relationship between pretax and after-tax returns achieved by mutual funds. Peterson, Pietranico, Riepe, and Xu (2002), however, found time-series persistence in after-tax returns of mutual funds, suggesting that investors may be able to predict, at least partly, which funds are apt to offer better after-tax returns in the future. In addition, they found empirical evidence that investment style (e.g., pursuing "value" stocks, pursuing "growth" stocks, market timing) and portfolio risk level are important determinants of after-tax returns. Surprisingly, they found that turnover is not a statistically significant determinant of after-tax returns. The reason may be that mutual funds explicitly designed to be "tax aware" may try to defer capital gains by reducing portfolio turnover or by increasing turnover in specifically tax-related transactions (e.g., tax-loss harvesting). An alternative explanation of this result is that the turnover levels for almost all the funds were well above the low levels (5–10 percent a year) below which tax deferral starts to have an important impact.

A clear alternative to standard mutual funds that is attractive to tax-sensitive investors is the "tax-aware index fund." The advantages of such a fund were first described by Garland (1997). In some markets that are particularly efficient, the average actively managed fund underperforms passive index funds. Once the additional costs of active management and taxes are considered, passive funds are a natural way to produce competitive returns in these markets while minimizing turnover so as to defer realization of capital gains. Note that some market indices are more suitable than others for this purpose. Value-oriented and small-capitalization equity indices often drop a stock from the index when it has gone up too much by their metrics, leading to forced realizations of capital gains.

---

[44]The agency problem arises because the more the investor trades, the more money the broker makes.

The vast majority of stock market indices are weighted by the company's market capitalization. Because economic equilibrium theories and models, such as the capital asset pricing model, assume that frictions such as transaction costs and taxes are nil, the market value–based portfolios may not be efficient in a world that includes taxable investors. Therefore, new forms of passive indices weighted by criteria other than capitalization may ultimately prove most beneficial for taxable investors (see Dammon 1988; Subrahmanyam 1998).

The simplistic answer to implementation of the desirable deferral of capital gains taxes is to never sell anything. For many family offices and trust companies, pseudopassive accounts have thus become the norm for accounts with low-cost-basis stock. By "pseudopassive," we mean that, unfortunately for investors, the accounts continue to be charged active management fees. The combination of effectively passive management and active fees dooms investors to consistently poor net returns.

For investors who prefer to allocate funds to actively managed strategies, investment managers must undertake to minimize the impact of taxation while continuing to pursue the active strategy for which they are being paid. Apelfeld, Granito, and Psarris (1996) showed that if asset managers have reasonable predictive skill (which they all purport to have), active strategies can be carried out in a tax-efficient fashion—through reducing turnover while intelligently realizing capital losses that can be used to offset realized capital gains.

Levels of Tax Awareness. Various levels of tax awareness and tax-aware strategies are discernible among investment management firms.

The most widespread practice with respect to taxes is to *ignore them altogether.* Most SMA programs use thousands of essentially identical accounts and require that incoming portfolios be liquidated (with large potential tax consequences) to fund the new portfolio. For investors in such portfolios, the only advantage of a separate account over a public mutual fund is the ability to use capital losses generated in the account to offset capital gains realized on other investments. This benefit is not trivial. Because U.S. mutual funds cannot distribute capital losses to their investors, a mutual fund investor would have to liquidate the holdings to realize a capital loss for tax purposes.

A slightly more tax-aware approach is for each individual account to copy a model portfolio that is managed with some degree of tax awareness, which can lead to effective deferral of capital gains taxes. This approach still requires liquidation of incoming security portfolios, creating the same potentially large tax consequences. And it is still suboptimal because investors will have different cost bases in their positions and other heterogeneities. No single investor will have the "average" tax circumstances purportedly represented by the model portfolio. The major advantage of such an account over a tax-aware mutual fund is that it allows tax losses to pass through to the investor without account liquidation.

A common practice among bank trust departments and family offices that routinely service HNW investors is to ignore taxes for the first 50 weeks of the tax year and, then, to do a manual year-end review of portfolio gains and losses. Selected positions with capital losses are sold at year-end to offset, at least partially, capital gains that may have been taken during the tax year as a result of routine portfolio transactions. Proceeds of year-end tax sales are then invested in new securities or "parked" in an exchange traded fund (ETF) during any applicable "wash sale" period and later reinvested in the same securities that had been subject to year-end sale.[45] At best, this process is a labor-intensive one that ignores the opportunities for tax-efficient investment transactions throughout the rest of the tax year.

A more sophisticated approach is to use a model account but use rule-based methods to prevent "tax dumb" transactions in individual accounts. For example, one could set a rule that a position with a short-term capital gain should never be sold. Rule-based methods can be applied to preexisting holdings when a new account is started, but to "migrate" preexisting accounts in a consistently rational fashion is difficult without considering explicit economic trade-offs (e.g., taxes) and risk–return expectations. In addition, rules must be customized to each manager's style (e.g., value versus growth, low turnover, high turnover, trading urgency, typical liquidity) or the rules can easily interfere with investment strategies.

Many firms are reluctant to use rule-based approaches because of the potential for client dissatisfaction when a rule prevents an investment manager from acting on a judgment that subsequently proves correct. For example, suppose an investment analyst covering Company XYZ stock believes the stock will fall substantially in value in the near future. The portfolio managers respond by selling XYZ stock out of tax-exempt accounts. If the firm has a rule against realizing short-term gains, XYZ will continue to be held in taxable accounts, however, where a sale would realize a short-term gain. If the stock does fall as predicted, clients that were forced by the rule to keep the position in XYZ may be unhappy. They may be hard to convince that the investment firm was prudent to hold XYZ to avoid realization of the capital gain.

Full exploitation of loss harvesting is becoming a popular technique. As described by Arnott, Berkin, and Ye (2001), tax-loss harvesting involves forming a rule that requires a security position to be sold when its price falls below the cost basis by a threshold percentage. To the extent that the returns of the securities in a portfolio have cross-sectional dispersion, the portfolio is apt to have some positions with losses, even when the portfolio has produced a positive return overall. The capital losses arising from loss harvesting can then be used to offset capital gains realized in the same portfolio, to offset capital gains realized in another portfolio held by the same investor, or to carry forward (with some limitations) to offset gains

---

[45] See Part II for wash sale rules.

realized in future tax years (see Part II). The economic value of the tax deferral achieved through loss harvesting must always be weighed against the transaction costs needed to undertake loss-harvesting trades that would otherwise not be required for investment reasons. In addition, loss harvesting may not be compatible with some active management styles. For example, an active value manager may find stocks increasingly attractive as they fall in price. A loss-harvesting rule would force the sale of many securities at the precise moment they are considered most attractive by this manager.

The properties that would be desirable in any particular approach for large-scale tax-aware portfolio management would include the following:

- Explicit economic trade-offs among expectations of return, risk, taxes, and trading costs should be allowed.
- Beyond taxes, other forms of portfolio customization should be supported (e.g., different risk preferences and constraints).
- The ability to use tax lot–by–tax lot information to minimize taxes should be supported.
- The tax management process should inhibit the implementation of active management strategies as little as possible.
- The process should be algorithmic in nature so that it can be substantially automated. In this way, a large number of portfolios can be efficiently handled in a quality-controlled fashion.

Tax Overlays. An increasingly important aspect of portfolio manufacturing lies in choosing a middle ground between passive and active management for taxable investors. Such processes are often called "tax overlay" or "cloning." An overlay strategy works in a way that is similar to a tax-aware passive index fund. The index fund is managed so as to closely mirror the return and risk characteristics of a published index that is presumed to offer efficient return–risk trade-offs. Many index fund portfolios will not hold exactly the constituents of the index, but will concentrate the portfolio in a smaller number of liquid securities. The fund weights the positions to mirror the overall characteristics of the published index. Similarly, the tax-aware index fund may vary from the exact index constituents in an effort to defer net capital gains that may arise through changes in the membership of the index.

In a tax overlay, the procedure is essentially the same as in the tax-aware index fund but the portfolio tries to mirror something other than a published index. Many investment firms construct a model portfolio that, given the nature of their typical client, encompasses their beliefs about the best investment portfolio available. Tax optimization can then be used to customize the model portfolio to the tax circumstances of each particular investor.

The overlay process has a number of attractive qualities. First, the model portfolio need not be constructed by any quantitative process but can be built on any investment process that a particular firm uses. So, investment firms with strong fundamentals-based (rather than quantitative) approaches can continue to do what they believe they do well; the model portfolio embodies investment views without expressing those beliefs in a numerical form. Because the strategy involves overlays, it also allows investment firms to use historically successful funds—with audited and published track records—as models. This information gives investors an understanding of what they are investing in and its potential risks and returns.

In addition, use of a model portfolio can clarify the value of tax-deferral procedures because it creates a procedural distinction between active management and tax management. To highlight the value added by active management, the model portfolio (adjusted for assumed trading costs) can be measured against an appropriate published benchmark. The client's individual portfolio can be measured against the model portfolio on an after-tax basis to measure the value of tax awareness. Such a separation does not imply that a successful active portfolio combined with an efficient tax overlay will necessarily be better for investors than a tax-aware passive fund, but it allows a clearer investigation of the issue than the passive fund strategy allows.

Overlay procedures sidestep a frequent criticism of optimization techniques—namely, that errors in the return and risk estimates that are inputs to the optimization procedures can lead to portfolio weightings that are unintuitive—and sometimes irrational. The process provides the labor efficiency of automation but avoids this issue. To the extent that overlay procedures are themselves passive (they simply try to match the model portfolio), they do not require estimation of expected returns.[46]

Other Overlays. The overlay process can be used to handle a wide variety of heterogeneities in addition to taxes. For example, consider a firm that wishes to use a successful mutual fund as the model portfolio. Mutual funds may invest in hundreds of securities, which might be impractical for an HNW portfolio of a few million dollars. So, the firm might establish an overlay to the tax optimization procedure framed as follows: "Once a month, adjust Mr. X's portfolio to look as similar as possible to the model portfolio while minimizing taxes, subject to the condition of not having more than 50 stocks." Similarly, the overlay process can incorporate customized risk aversion for a conservative investor, an aggressive investor, or one who has different (from typical) attitudes about the relative importance of market-relative and absolute risk.

---

[46]Numerous authors have found (e.g., Best and Grauer 1991; Chopra and Ziemba 1993) that the majority of suboptimal portfolio weights arise from errors in expected returns rather than errors in expected variances or correlations.

Even specific client constraints, such as "never buy stock in the company I work for" or "no utilities with nuclear power," can be easily accommodated in this framework. Not only can such an optimization process automatically handle such exclusions, but it can make substitutions of other securities as required to follow the model portfolio most efficiently.

Treating Taxes as a Transaction Cost. A key advance in the development of tax-aware portfolio management strategies was put forward by Apelfeld, Fowler, and Gordon (1996). Rather than try to estimate after-tax total returns on assets, they adjusted expected returns only for taxes on income. They explicitly modeled capital gains taxes as a form of transaction cost levied on position-closing trades—usually, sales. They modeled different tax lots of the same security as different securities so that different capital gains taxes could be applied to the different lots. The portfolio could then be subjected to the same sort of mean–variance portfolio optimization used by many quantitatively oriented managers for tax-exempt portfolios. The goal of this effort was to integrate the loss-harvesting strategy with an active or passive portfolio management process.

In this approach, capital losses are not harvested on the basis of a rule; the realization of tax losses and the potential offset against capital gains arises from the inputs of all the securities in the subject portfolio, including expected return, risk, and trading cost. For example, consider a situation in which the portfolio manager has a "sell" rating on a stock on which she will realize a large capital gain. The optimization procedure searches the portfolio for another stock with a potential capital loss and a "neutral" or "sell" rating. The manager sells both positions and thereby offsets the capital gain with the capital loss. The manager can then invest the proceeds of the two sales in new positions with "buy" ratings.

This simple example is easily understood, but what about a realistic HNW portfolio that contains 50–200 tax lots? Clearly, finding the set of the most desirable transactions among the millions of possible combinations of multiple trades requires significant computational power.

Since the late 1990s, a number of algorithms (and numerous refinements of them) based on the "taxes as trading costs" idea have been developed to mechanically balance risk, return, and tax expectations. The most important concept to emerge is that capital gains taxes need to be amortized over time to allow the proper trade-offs among return, risk, and reduction or deferral of taxes. In the procedure, taxes on income are incorporated as adjustments to expected returns. For example, if the expected income yield on a particular stock in the portfolio is 3 percent and the expected income yield on the benchmark index is 2 percent, the tax on income will consume a larger portion of the expected return from that security. If we assume a 40 percent tax on income, the adjustment to benchmark relative expected return would be (−40 percent × 1 percent) = −0.4 percent.

Taxes on capital gains are treated as a trading cost but are amortized (i.e., converted to units of annualized return) over a long period that reflects the expected holding period of the security that will replace the one being sold, as well as other factors. Estimating the appropriate amortization rate for capital gains taxes can be complex. Among the potential considerations are the following:

- Although linear amortization is a sufficiently close approximation for small costs, such as trading commissions, estimates of a potentially large tax impact will not usually be accurate when linear approximations are used. The tax impact ought to be thought of *geometrically* because $(1 - 0.01) \times (1 + 0.01) = 0.999$, which is close to 1 whereas $(1 - 0.40) \times (1 + 0.40) = 0.84$, which is not close to 1. Trading a 1 percent cost today for a 1 percent improvement in return for one year will produce almost the same amount of wealth in a year. On the other hand, trading a 40 percent cost today for a 40 percent improvement in return for one year will result in significantly less wealth in a year.

- Deferring a transaction until a short-term gain becomes a long-term gain represents a true decrease in taxes. The *incremental* tax on short-term gain transactions should be amortized over the period from the present until that particular position would achieve long-term status.

- Because the compounding of returns allowed by tax deferral is important, long-term amortization rates should reflect the compounding benefit of tax deferral as well as the probability of escaping capital gains taxes at death.

- Limitations on tax-loss carryforwards may affect amortization rates. If the portfolio's value reflects the presence of a large number of unrealized losses that cannot be carried forward into future tax years, it may benefit the investor to change the amortization rate to encourage realizing some gains now rather than lose the economic value of the unrealized losses.

An important element of overlay procedures is recognition that model portfolios will not reflect any specific investor's concerns about market-relative and absolute risk. This weakness can be addressed by forming a modified model portfolio that includes an appropriate weight in cash.

Overlay procedures also introduce a form of "dual benchmark" problem. Suppose a firm's model portfolio is benchmarked to some published index (e.g., the Russell 1000 Index or the MSCI Europe/Australasia/Far East Index) and is likely to resemble that index to a large degree. The "cloned" portfolios are supposed to resemble the model portfolio, but after all the overlay changes, how does the manager ensure that actual investor portfolios also bear sufficient resemblance to the underlying published index? For example, the model portfolio may be tilted away from the published index toward a larger percentage of small-cap stocks. By virtue of tax optimization, however, an investor's individual portfolio might accidentally take an even larger tilt toward small-cap stocks, which might be viewed as excessive relative to the published index. Wang (1999) provides a detailed treatment of this issue.

Dealing with a Legacy Portfolio

Another frequent concern when managing the assets of HNW clients is how to deal with the preexisting (legacy) portfolio of a new client. Portfolio transition strategies can easily be illustrated in the overlay framework. At one extreme, the investor can simply keep the existing portfolio, which obviously creates no new net capital gains. At the other extreme, the investor can liquidate his or her current portfolio and purchase the firm's model portfolio, perhaps adapted for differences in risk aversion or other constraints. This approach is apt to lead to significant capital gains taxes. For intermediate cases, one can construct a "tax versus tracking error to the model" efficient frontier by running the optimization across a spectrum of various levels of risk aversion. For each value of risk aversion, a different optimal solution will result, with each solution placing a different emphasis in the trade-off between taxes and risk. By incorporating loss harvesting, the manager can often move an existing portfolio toward the model portfolio with no net capital gains— even perhaps with net capital losses. But this strategy is not without cost because, to the extent that losses harvested could have been used to offset involuntary gains, a dollar-for-dollar trade-off is forgone in tax savings.

Dealing with concentrated positions in a preexisting portfolio is another task that often arises in a large investment firm. One procedure that has been successfully implemented in the portfolio manufacturing context is the following:

1. Borrow against the concentrated holding to the extent allowable by margin requirements. Fund a "complementary" portfolio (see Chapter 10) that hedges the concentrated holding with a broadly diversified portfolio of volatile stocks relative to a particular stock index (i.e., the S&P 500 Index).

2. Short index futures or ETFs (the choice will affect loss harvesting of short-term losses in the complementary portfolio) to put the exposure to market risk (but not exposure to other risk or return factors) back to the original level.

3. Carry out loss harvesting in the complementary portfolio. These losses can then offset gains realized by selling off pieces of the concentrated position. If the market falls, the hedge position will gain value. (It may pay to harvest some short-term losses that can be carried forward to offset the realization of this possible eventual gain.)

4. Reinvest the proceeds from all sales of both the complementary portfolio and the concentrated position back into the complementary portfolio.

Over time, the portfolio will gradually transition out of the concentrated position at an accelerating rate while taxes are deferred in a controlled manner. Determining the appropriate balance between risk control and tax savings is discussed in detail in Chapter 10 and also in Stein, Siegel, Narasimhan, and Appeadu (2000).

Multiperiod Analysis

A few more issues need to be considered in setting the parameters of portfolio construction and trading in the portfolio manufacturing context. Mean–variance optimization operates as a single-period model. It assumes that the future is one period. Therefore, at any given moment, the usual optimization procedures assume that whatever views one now holds about expected returns and risk will be held forever. If transaction costs are zero, however, the lack of realism in this assumption is of little consequence because the manager can continuously adjust the portfolio as her or his beliefs change through time at no cost.

This attitude is clearly unrealistic in the context of taxable HNW portfolios. Broadie (1993), Chopra (1993), and Markowitz and Van Dijk (2003) have suggested that, given the potential for future changes in views, investors are indifferent to whether a portfolio is exactly optimal based on current views. Investors operate on the principle that a portfolio can be "close enough" to optimal. As long as a portfolio is "close enough," investors simply leave it alone.

Defining *how close* to optimal is close enough is mathematically complex for all but trivial cases, but such statistical techniques as resampling (a form of Monte Carlo simulation) can be used to numerically estimate the indifference region. This process not only leads to a reduction in unnecessary turnover but also adds an important benefit to the portfolio manufacturing process: Different portfolios do not all have to be traded at the same time. If a manager has 10,000 portfolios under management, he can use an automated procedure to check each one daily for its closeness to optimality, thereby ensuring that no portfolio that needs attention is neglected. At the same time, the preponderance of portfolios will be in the indifference region, meaning that they will not require any action. This factor will tend to spread the trading of client portfolios across time, reducing the market impact of aggregated trades and reducing the labor intensity of operations.

Accommodating Investment Styles

Investment style plays an important role in the ability of a portfolio manufacturing process to enhance investors' after-tax returns. Index funds obviously offer the least turnover and hence are the easiest investment style on which to defer realization of capital gains. Among active strategies, quantitative approaches often provide more flexibility than fundamentals-based approaches because quantitative approaches allow a nearly infinite number of combinations of different stocks to be constructed to provide a desired set of portfolio characteristics—for example, a portfolio that is tilted toward small-cap stocks (relative to the S&P 500) but has the same sector weights as the S&P 500. Even fundamentals-based approaches can be accommodated if tax losses are sensibly harvested to offset capital gains when realizing a gain becomes necessary because of a negative opinion on an appreciated security. Value strategies—for example, tilting toward stocks with low price-to-earnings ratios or low market value to book value—can be more difficult in terms of tax deferral because they naturally promote selling appreciated securities. Strategies driven by price momentum do the opposite.

The portfolio manufacturing concept can be extended to accommodate complex strategies involving multiple asset managers or multiple related accounts. Many HNW investors have chosen to diversify their portfolios among managers. Some financial services firms even offer preselected packages of several managers (known as "multiple disciplinary accounts," or MDAs), each specializing in a different part of the markets. Unfortunately, having multiple accounts among several active managers can lead to inefficient investing because the sum of the various subportfolios may be similar to the makeup of a passive index. The result is an index portfolio that suffers from both active management fees and unnecessary trading costs as different managers take offsetting actions. In addition, if the manager universes are not mutually exclusive, inadvertent wash sales are also possible because no manager is likely to be aware of what the others are doing.

A better way to include complex strategies is to have each of the multiple managers provide a model portfolio, each of which has its own benchmark. The selection universe for the model portfolios may or may not be overlapping, but the client's actual portfolio is traded as a *single*, central account. The individual manager portfolios are simply model portfolios, and no effort is made to make separate trades for "sleeves" (subaccounts). The goal in this situation is to perform a "global" optimization of the client's portfolio that is tax efficient across all of the managers and captures as much of the investment performance of the model portfolios as possible.

An even easier way to include complex strategies is to form a benchmark that combines the model portfolios, with each position weighted proportionally to the hypothetical fraction that each model portfolio constitutes of the entire benchmark portfolio. In this case, if Manager X is supposed to be 30 percent of the market value of the MDA and has a 4 percent position in IBM, the benchmark has a 1.2 percent (0.3×0.04) position in IBM. At this point, a simple "minimum variance" optimization of the existing positions against this benchmark will provide the tax optimization.

Unfortunately, this simple method is appropriate only when the multiple model accounts have mutually distinct universes of securities. Consider the following example of what happens when the positions overlap. An MDA has two managers, each with 50 percent of the investor's capital. Manager A thinks Exxon Mobil Corporation is a great stock and overweights it 3 percent. She has the market weighting for the airline sector. Manager B has a 5 percent overweight in airlines, which he considers undervalued, and he overweights Exxon 3 percent as a hedge against oil prices rising. If the MDA manager simply adds the positions together, the result will be 3 percent overweight in Exxon and a 2.5 percent overweight in airlines. But Manager B wanted to overweight Exxon as a hedge against his big airline bet. Because the airline sector is now overweighted only 2.5 percent, Manager B ought to want to overweight Exxon only 1.5 percent as a hedge (keep the same 5-to-3 ratio). So, the preferred overweight in Exxon ought to be 3 percent for Manager A and 1.5 percent for Manager B. Instead, a 2.25 percent, not 3 percent, overweight in Exxon becomes the correct "benchmark" (joint model portfolio) weight.[47]

A more sophisticated way to handle the MDA case is becoming increasingly popular among large *institutions* that use multiple managers. They follow the procedure outlined in diBartolomeo (1999) on running a central portfolio with multiple model portfolios as inputs. Essentially, this process involves each manager making inferences about the "implied" alpha for each stock. The central portfolio's manager can then weight the alpha values of the managers on the basis of their assigned weights in the central portfolio. Given the "consensus alphas," the central portfolio manager can optimize the portfolio in the conventional fashion. Numerous other advantages of the approach, enumerated in the original paper, can reduce costs and taxes and potentially improve the effectiveness of active management.

Why Shortcuts Won't Work

Portfolio manufacturing comes with some important caveats. The first is that it requires appropriate resources—in terms of investment professionals and analytical systems to undertake the key role of customizing the firm's investment products and beliefs to the needs and wants of each individual investor. Customization requires skills, tools, and experience that are quite distinct from the competent analysis of securities and financial markets.

The second caveat pertains to a dangerous issue in the manufacturing approach, which is the natural desire to oversimplify the complexities of managing investments for HNW individuals for the sake of extending operational efficiencies. The underlying economics of investing under taxation and a variety of other heterogeneous circumstances demand that investment professionals resist the temptation to take shortcuts. *Most prevalent among the ill-advised shortcuts is*: ignoring the actual economic circumstances of investors entirely and organizing "optimal" portfolio formation around simple sets of constraints.

For example, an investment firm might offer a product organized as follows: "Take a list of 50 stocks that our firm views favorably. Form a portfolio that includes as many of them as possible, subject to the conditions that no one stock be more than 4 percent of the portfolio and that there be at least 20 stocks in the portfolio. Limit turnover such that the portfolio does not generate net capital gains each year in excess of 10 percent of the portfolio value at the beginning of the calendar year." At first

---

[47] Similar distortions can occur even if the selection universes are mutually exclusive if one manager is much more aggressive than another.

glance, such a plan does not seem unreasonable. The critical issue of balancing risk and taxes is handled in the crudest possible way, however, by simply ensuring some basic diversification and limiting tax realizations to an amount that might appear modest to investors. A detailed understanding of what portfolio specification actually makes the most sense for an individual investor is entirely missing.

A more subtle, but equally unsatisfactory, shortcut was exemplified by a certain successful institutional asset management firm that was quantitatively oriented. To get started managing for HNW investors, this otherwise sophisticated firm simply took its existing institutional equity portfolio and ran it through an optimization process designed to defer taxes. In simulations, the approach was successful in reducing the degree of net realized gains, at the cost of a modest decrease in active returns. The firm gave no thought, however, to the heterogeneous nature of the investors or to their different (as compared with tax-exempt institutions) preferences with respect to absolute and market-relative risks. Without a readiness to adjust its strategy to fit the varying needs of HNW investors, this firm found little acceptance among individual investors, and the entire effort was eventually abandoned. A "one size fits all" approach, even if derived from a sophisticated strategy that had been successful with institutional investors, is apt to fail.

Many individual investors do not understand what is in their own best interests. The portfolio manufacturing paradigm does not relieve investment professionals of the obligation to educate their clients sufficiently that the firm can make appropriate, well-thought-out choices about the parameterization of the portfolio management process. H.L. Mencken said, "For every complex problem, there is a solution that is simple, neat, and wrong."

Summary

"Portfolio manufacturing" is a concept dealing with how an investment firm should organize its activities so as to provide high-quality services appropriate to the heterogeneous needs of HNW investors in a cost-effective fashion. Many, although not all, of the differences among HNW investors revolve around taxes. Tax-aware investing considers

*   balancing the need to sell appreciated securities for investment reasons (diversification, security selection) against the need to not sell them for tax reasons,
*   balancing the need to sell at a loss for tax reasons against the need to not sell them for investment reasons, and
*   harmonizing the purchases and sales within tax periods.

Part IV
Special Topics

How to locate stocks and bonds among tax-advantaged and ordinary portfolios has been a topic of controversy, so we provide separate treatment of it in Chapter 9. This topic is of considerable interest to those whose wealth is not many times larger than the amounts that can be set aside in individual retirement accounts, 401(k) plans, and so on. What to do with large proportions of wealth concentrated in a single asset with large unrealized capital gains is of potential interest to private investors *across* the wealth spectrum. This question is addressed in some detail in Chapter 10. (Appendices A and B are included specifically for readers who want to gain a deeper understanding of the issues in those two chapters through a hands-on quantitative exercise. Appendix A is needed to follow the later example in Appendix B.) Finally, Chapter 11 includes a description—from the wealthy investor's viewpoint—of desirable features for any approach to benchmarking and assessing such an investor's investment management program.

9. Individual Retirement Plans and Location

One of the principal savings vehicles for individuals in the United States and many other countries is the individual retirement plan (IRP). These plans are often referred to as "defined-contribution" plans because the amount of money in the plan, which will be available (less taxes) to the participant, is based on a fixed contribution by the employee and/or plan sponsor, as increased by the investment returns in the fund. The investment performance risk is borne by the beneficiary.[48]

These kinds of plans are useful and valuable for high-net-worth (HNW) individuals in the lower ranks of wealth. For the very wealthy, the benefits may be worthwhile but are unlikely to make a material difference in overall wealth, so setting up and managing the plans may not be worth the effort. For sophisticated estate planning, these plans are even counterproductive in some circumstances. For example, transferring the economic value of IRPs out of one's estate can be very difficult. So, not everyone who qualifies for an IRP should use one.

IRPs (and some other tax-sheltering arrangements) create a new issue for asset management—namely, the *asset location* problem. HNW individuals will have assets located in tax-deferred vehicles and assets held (and taxed) directly in the name of the individual investor. Because the tax treatment of investments inside these plans is so different from the tax treatment of assets outside the plans, asset classes become functionally different on an after-tax basis.

Summary of U.S. Retirement Plans

In the United States, there are a number of IRP structures—known by a variety of designations. Each plan has different eligibility requirements for the individual and possibly the individual's employer. Each plan has different limitations on how much money can be contributed to the plan and on the extent to which those contributions will be tax advantaged. In most (not all) plans, both the monies contributed and the investment earnings are tax deferred until withdrawn. This characteristic is advantageous to the investor with respect to the compounding of investment returns on a pretax basis and has more potential benefits if the investor

---

[48]A defined-benefit plan fixes the amount of the benefit to be paid to the beneficiary, so the plan sponsor must provide enough in contributions that, with the investment returns, enough money will be available to pay the benefits. The investment risk is borne by the plan sponsor.

will be subject to lower marginal tax rates during their retirement years than their contribution years. Keep in mind that the very wealthy are unlikely to face a lower marginal tax rate in retirement.

The subsections that follow provide a brief overview of the U.S. plans as of the writing of this book.

Regular Individual Retirement Account. Almost every U.S. worker can, until approximately age 70 1/2, establish his or her own IRA plan. In this plan, an individual may contribute up to $4,000 a year.[49] People over age 50 can make small additional contributions. Depending on the individual's adjusted gross income, some or all of the monies earned to fund contributions is tax deferred for income tax purposes. Investment earnings within the plan are tax deferred. IRA planholders must begin to withdraw funds from their IRAs at age 70 1/2. Once withdrawals are under way, capital must be withdrawn according to a schedule of minimum annual rates. Monies withdrawn from IRA plans are subject to income tax at ordinary income rates. In addition, the plans impose a 10 percent penalty for withdrawals before age 59 1/2.

The income level of most HNW individuals severely limits tax-deferred contributions to regular IRAs. For HNW individuals, required withdrawal minimums may be counterproductive in estate planning.

Roth IRA. The Roth plan is similar to the regular IRA except that contributions are not tax deferred (i.e., not deductible in the contribution year). Withdrawals from Roth plans—whether arising from contributed funds or investment earnings—are free of federal income tax, however, if the plan owner is over age 59 1/2 and the account has been open for at least five years. Roth plans involve no mandatory withdrawals. The same 10 percent penalty exists as in regular IRAs for early withdrawals. Roth plans can be a good choice for individuals who believe they will be in a high marginal tax bracket during their retirement years. Therefore, these plans are usually appropriate for HNW individuals.

SIMPLE IRA. The SIMPLE IRA program helps small businesses (with fewer than 100 employees) offer a retirement plan with a minimum of paperwork. A regular IRA account is set up for each employee. Contributions to the account can be made in two ways. Either employers must match employee contributions up to 3 percent of employee compensation, or employers must make a contribution of at least 2 percent of compensation, even if the employee does not contribute.

SEP-IRA. This plan is designed for self-employed individuals and small businesses with a few employees. Employers can contribute up to 25 percent of an employee's compensation, up to a maximum of $42,000 per tax year, on a tax-deferred

---

[49] Starting in 2008, the limit will be $5,000 plus an inflation adjustment.

basis. Employees may contribute up to an additional $4,000, on a tax-deferred basis, if under age 59 1/2 or $4,500 if over age 59 1/2. Investment earnings of the plan are also tax deferred. Withdrawals made after age 59 1/2 are subject to normal income taxation. Withdrawals made before age 59 1/2 are subject to a 10 percent penalty, with certain exceptions. Withdrawals must begin by approximately age 70 1/2 and are subject to a schedule of annual minimum amounts.

Keogh Profit Sharing. This plan is designed for self-employed individuals and partnerships. Employers can contribute up to 25 percent of an employee's compensation up to a maximum of $42,000 per tax year on a tax-deferred basis. Investment earnings of the plan are tax deferred. Employee ownership of the value of the plan account may be subject to a vesting schedule defined by the employer. Employees may not contribute to a Keogh plan. Upon voluntary or involuntary termination of employment, employees may roll over the vested portion of a Keogh plan to a different plan under their personal control (i.e., an IRA). Withdrawals may begin at age 59 1/2 and must begin by 1 April of the year in which the participant became age 70 1/2. Distributions are subject to normal income taxation. The usual 10 percent penalty applies to withdrawals made before age 59 1/2.

401(k). The 401(k) plan is the fastest growing type of defined-contribution plan. In a 401(k) plan, employees agree to defer part of their compensation, up to prescribed limits, to place in the plan. As of 2006, employees below age 50 may have up to $15,000 annually ($20,000 if over age 50) of their compensation directed into the plan on a tax-deferred basis. Investment earnings while capital is in the plan are tax deferred. Because monies directed into a 401(k) plan are considered a deferral of compensation, these monies are also free of the federal contributions required to the U.S. Social Security system and Medicare. Employers can also match employee contributions to 401(k) programs up to prescribed limits or choose to make non-elective contributions, even if the employee does not contribute. Contributions by employers are subject to "fairness rules" that limit the extent to which contributions for more highly compensated employees may be larger than the contributions to employees of lower compensation levels. Employers can also make provisions in the 401(k) plan to allow employees to borrow money from the 401(k) for certain purposes, such as purchasing a home. Withdrawals from 401(k) plans are subject to ordinary income taxes. Penalties may be levied on withdrawals before age 59 1/2. Distributions must begin by approximately age 70 1/2 and are subject to a schedule of minimum annual amounts. Effective 1 January 2006, investors may designate all or part of their 401(k) contributions to be treated in the Roth format, which allows many individuals to increase the amounts contributed under Roth status.

403(b)(7). This plan is similar to the 401(k) salary-deferral plan but is targeted to nonprofit organizations, such as educational institutions, hospitals, and religious organizations. As of 2006, employees may have up to $15,000 (if the employee is under age 50) or $20,000 (if over age 50) of their compensation directed into the plan on a tax-deferred basis each year. These limits increase to $15,000 (under age 50) and to $20,000 (over age 50) in 2006. Investment earnings while capital is in the plan are tax deferred. Withdrawals may begin at the age of 59 1/2 under normal circumstances but may start at age 55 in the event of employment termination (voluntary or involuntary) or disability. Withdrawals must begin by approximately age 70 1/2 and are subject to a schedule of minimum annual distributions. Distributions are taxed at ordinary income rates. A 10 percent penalty is applied to early withdrawals before age 59 1/2 (with the exceptions for termination or disability).

Suitability of Plans for Various Wealth Levels

For very wealthy individual investors, individual retirement plans will form only a small part of overall investment assets and the plans are not typically required to support consumption during retirement years. A key issue for the plans of these HNW investors is estate planning. Obviously, if IRP assets can be passed to heirs as part of an estate, overall taxation will be lower for an IRP than if one were to distribute the funds from the retirement plan, pay taxes on the distributions, and then pass the previously taxed distributions to heirs as part of an estate. A variety of legislative proposals have been made to change the rules on mandatory minimum distributions so as to alleviate this problem in the future.

For investors for whom no estate tax will be due because they are below the exemption amount, retirement accounts can transmute high-yielding, highly taxed investments into tax-exempt investments because no tax is paid within the accounts and no tax is paid at the time of death. Beware, however, that mandatory distribution requirements affect this potential benefit.

For individuals with substantial income but little in accumulated investment capital, the need to fund consumption during retirement can be a major issue. As a rule of thumb, financial planning experts suggest that individuals will require a postretirement income of 75–80 percent of their preretirement income to maintain a comparable lifestyle. Although some portion of this required income is likely to come from government-funded pension schemes, such as Social Security, individuals of moderate net worth should make every effort to take maximum advantage of the tax deferral offered by individual retirement plans.

Asset Location

Whether to hold particular investment assets in a retirement account or not is a complex problem involving a host of variables that are difficult to estimate and, in the case of tax rates, subject to abrupt change.

Tax Aspects. The importance of retirement accounts is primarily to achieve tax deferral, the value of which is described throughout this book. *Whether a contribution to the account is made with after-tax money (and tax-free on withdrawal) or the contribution is made with pretax money (and taxed on withdrawal) is not key to the value of these accounts.* The reason is that the tax payment is mathematically identical to a single-period negative return and thus has the same effect on the geometric mean return whether it occurs at the beginning or at the end. But when the investor's estate will not be subject to tax (because it is less than the exemption amount), the ideal plan is one in which contributions are pretax, not after tax, because all taxes will be avoided—*now and in the future.*

In addition to the tax-deferral effect, investors are quite likely to be in a lower marginal income tax rate bracket when they are withdrawing funds from rather than depositing funds into their retirement accounts. Marginal income tax rates have fluctuated greatly since the establishment of the U.S. federal income tax, however, so there is no assurance that the future prevailing tax rates, even in lower income brackets, will be lower than the investor's tax rate at the time the funds are being placed in tax-deferred retirement accounts. In addition, many HNW investors will have sufficient income during their postretirement years that no decline in marginal tax rate ought to be expected.

Another important aspect arises when the total applicable tax rate is lower for investments held outside the retirement account than for those flowing through it. For example, long-term capital gains and dividends are taxed at a {15 percent} rate outside retirement plans, but although gains and dividends are not taxed while in the retirement plans, the money withdrawn will be taxed as ordinary income, which for most wealthy U.S. investors, means at the {35 percent} rate.[50] The correct analysis is not so simple, however, because with extremely long deferral times (e.g., multiple decades), the higher exit tax rate may be so diluted by the benefits of tax deferral that using an IRP is still economically advantageous. One cannot simply assume that a higher tax rate on withdrawal relative to the applicable tax rate on the same investment return held outside the IRP makes the IRP unattractive. It depends.

Losses in traditional IRAs can be used to offset gains only when all the individual's IRAs combined have been distributed—essentially in a complete liquidation of all the combined retirement account holdings—because the gains and losses are netted. Therefore, interim tax-loss harvesting is not possible. Although

---

[50]Recall that tax rates and other statutory values in the tax code are shown in braces, { }.

investors may wish to put some risky, highly volatile investments in their IRAs for nontax reasons (because these investments may constitute some part of any portfolio), doing so provides no tax advantage like the advantage that comes from accounts in which one can deduct a loss.

Nontax Aspects. Generally, the more tax inefficient the investment is relative to other investments the investor owns, the better off that tax-inefficient investment is in a retirement account. Keep in mind, however, that a key factor in asset location is the need for liquidity to deal with unexpected consumption expenditures. Other factors that can be relevant to the decision include the investor's life expectancy, existing portfolio holdings, embedded capital gains, and the available wealth levels in both the taxable and tax-deferred accounts.

Which Asset Classes to Hold in Retirement Accounts. A dynamic programming method for analyzing asset location was developed by Dammon, Spatt, and Zhang (2004). They came to the following important conclusions:

- The relative attractiveness of taxable and tax-exempt bonds is conditional on the availability of a tax-deferred vehicle for holding the bonds. In essence, asset location and asset allocation form a single joint decision.
- In the absence of other factors (e.g., asset allocation constraints), when the tax rate on dividends is lower than the tax rate on interest and is identical to the long-term capital gains tax rate, holding stocks in the retirement account is not worthwhile. (Presumably, this reasoning does not apply when substantial portions of the expected capital gains on stocks are short term and highly taxed.)
- For most investors, even relatively tax-inefficient stock investments (e.g., most mutual funds) should be kept outside the retirement account.
- Investors who hold bonds in their retirement account can benefit from holding a balanced portfolio of bonds and equities outside the tax-deferred accounts. Investors who hold a balanced portfolio inside their tax-deferred accounts can benefit from holding an all-equity portfolio outside the retirement accounts. The structure of holding equities and bonds in the tax-deferred retirement account *and* holding equities and bonds outside the tax-deferred account is generally unsuitable.
- Taxable bonds should almost always be held in retirement accounts. Only those investors seriously concerned about large, unanticipated "shocks" to their consumption (such as an enormous medical bill) that will require liquidity will find much advantage in holding taxable bonds outside the retirement account. HNW individuals typically have much higher consumption than the average investor, so the limits on the amount in a retirement account may make even this concern moot.

A study by Sialm and Shoven (2004) came to many similar conclusions. Their research also found that taxable bonds should be held in the tax-deferred retirement account. They argued that equities held outside the tax-deferred account should be selected to be tax efficient, such as index funds or "tax-aware" funds, whereas traditional actively managed funds should go inside the retirement account. Another extensive treatment of tax-advantaged savings vehicles can be found in Horan (2005).

Appendix A discusses a method for customizing location decisions and is necessary for the reader to understand the concentrated risk example in Appendix B.

Rebalancing

If stocks are held outside the retirement account and taxable bonds are held within the account, stocks are likely to outgrow the investor's target asset allocation. Therefore, some rebalancing will be necessary. When the rebalancing factor is considered, the conclusions about asset location may be somewhat contrary to the advice of the leading commentators cited in the last section.

Rebalancing usually requires selling stocks and buying bonds, which triggers taxable gains for stocks held directly and thereby increases the tax inefficiency of stocks, which can make it worth at least considering holding some stocks in a retirement account. But at {15 percent} for long-term capital gains, the tax rates are so favorable that selling the stocks may not be a material issue, especially when the tax is compared with the {35 percent} rate on bond interest. When the retirement account assets are small relative to the investor's total assets, as is common with very wealthy investors, the potential to bring about a material rebalancing in the retirement account may be small.

Summary

Retirement accounts, although nearly universally recommended by investment advisors, are not for everyone—especially very wealthy individuals. Whenever IRPs are considered, attention needs to be given to

- potential changes in future tax rates,
- trade-offs between low current tax rates and higher deferred withdrawal tax rates,
- the potential need for cash before withdrawals can be made without penalties,
- the likelihood of gain recognition even for low-tax-rate investments, and
- the relationship between the retirement account and the estate plan.

In summary, asset allocation and asset location for individual investors involve a holistic consideration of which assets are to be held inside and outside the retirement account in light of the likely tax consequences. The approach involves considering the timing of the person's needs for cash, the benefits of tax deferral, relative tax rates, and issues of rebalancing.

10. On Concentrated Risk

Wealthy investors are often vexed by the question of whether to diversify a large portion of their wealth that is concentrated in a single stock or business interest, especially when a substantial capital gains tax will need to be paid if they do. Investors may reasonably prefer to have the lower risk associated with a diversified portfolio but also prefer not to pay taxes. The challenge is how to decide how much to pay in tax to diversify.

Doing nothing accomplishes nothing with respect to lowering the risks of a portfolio that is concentrated in a small number of assets, nor does it provide the opportunity for consumption or reinvestment into more attractive opportunities. The tax code prohibits or severely limits how much in short sales against the box (shorting securities one owns), or closely related hedges, one can perform without triggering a capital gains tax event through a "constructive sale."[51] The result has been increasing complexity as investors find new approaches and the U.S. government passes new laws and regulations designed to close off the exceptions.

An approach to deciding how much of concentrated risk to alleviate through an outright sale is given in Appendix B. A better understanding of its mechanisms will result if the reader first masters the simpler example in Appendix A.

Proactive alternatives to reducing concentrated risk without triggering taxes use some combination of three principles: borrowing, "complementarity," and pooling. Hedging transactions—such as an offsetting short-sale or a tight "collar" combining a put and a call on the appreciated stock (and thus substantially removing both the possibility of loss and the opportunity for gain)—are considered constructive sales and do trigger taxes in the United States.

Borrowing

A common approach is to use borrowed funds. To avoid increasing overall risk, investors can use specially constructed transactions, such as short sales on related securities or on the market, "collars," or collar-containing "prepaid variable forwards" (PVFs). These techniques provide intermediate-term benefits but may involve long-term adverse tax treatment and high fees. The diversification benefits may be outweighed by additional hidden risks incurred through a combination of leverage and hedging positions. For example, because of the asymmetrical tax treatments of the instruments that make up a PVF collar, the minimum-risk hedge ratios derived from after-tax analysis are different from those derived on a pretax basis.

---

[51] For more information, see www.irs.gov.

Leverage, Short Sales, and Tax-Loss Harvesting. When an investor's concentrated position is only a part of the investor's investment portfolio, the advisor can restructure the remainder of the portfolio to offset the risk of continuing to hold the concentrated position (see the "Complementarity" section). When the concentrated position is held at a large capital gain and is all, or nearly all of the investor's portfolio, however, more aggressive steps may be appropriate. One approach for these cases is to use a combination of leverage, short sales, and tax-loss harvesting. The investor borrows on margin against the concentrated stock position and offsets the leveraged market risk by taking a short-sale position, not on the specific security (which would constitute a constructive sale), but on either an exchange-traded fund or a market index futures contract. The net funds generated are invested in a diversified portfolio of stocks with high specific risk (above-average return volatility) and a below-average correlation with overall market returns.

This approach will increase the likelihood of effective tax-loss harvesting, irrespective of market direction, through a high degree of dispersion in the return cross-section. Because the risks of a concentrated position are largely asset specific by definition, this diverse portfolio will also have low correlation with the concentrated position. A program of tax-loss harvesting in this diversifying portfolio will produce tax losses that can then be used to offset taxable gains created by concurrent sales of the concentrated position. Proceeds from sales of the concentrated position can then be reinvested into the diversifying portfolio, accelerating the entire process.

Over time, the concentrated position will be gradually sold off, with reduced realization of taxable capital gains. In addition, the diversifying portfolio may produce short-term loss realizations that offset short-term gains of any profit on the hedge. This approach can be achieved with low initial costs. As the concentrated position is sold off, however, the tax-loss harvesting may not generate sufficient tax losses to cover hedging profits that could arise in a long-term market decline. The expected value of the net benefit depends on specific investor circumstances.

Collars. In a collar, rather than hold a short position on the market, the investor can reduce risk more directly by purchasing an out-of-the-money long-term put option on the concentrated security holding. The purchase is financed through the sale of an out-of-the-money call option. Because of its customized nature, such a transaction makes the most sense for large amounts. Once overall risk has been reduced, borrowing against the portfolio becomes safer.

What are the complications? The first is that the strategy can be expensive. Customized options incur large dealer spreads, and they must be renewed at intervals, each time with a fee. Also, out-of-the-money puts are generally priced higher than out-of-the-money calls, implying that the investor must give up more upside return than the downside protection obtained to make the transaction self-financing. Second, so-called straddles create tax asymmetries that can negate the tax benefits of trying to avoid realizing gains on the original security. In essence, if prices move outside the collar, the hedging gain is taxed at a high short-term gains rate. But if the process produces a hedging loss after two years, the tax write-off is at the long-term rate. And it cannot be taken until the transaction is completed at the end of the five-year (or similar) period or when the position is closed out. This asymmetry introduces an unintended volatility risk.

Prepaid Variable Forward. A forward contract avoids the limitation in the two previous approaches: government limits on margin borrowing. The investor contracts with a counterparty to deliver the concentrated stock shares at a forward date. This forward sale (carefully written as a sale rather than a loan, to avoid margin restrictions) generates cash. The ability of the investor to deliver the shares is reinforced by a collar—the purchase of an out-of-the-money put financed by the sale of an out-of-the-money call. To avoid having the forward transaction characterized as a constructive sale, the terms are contingent on a formula specified in such a way that the outcome has some risk, and the associated put and call strike prices must be materially different. No statutory "safe harbor" has established how far apart the prices must be, although some professionals advise 20 percent. This PVF approach has the same complications as the collar, which it includes, plus additional fees.

Complementarity

Another technique is to construct a "complementary fund" in the form of a portfolio purposely diversified to offset the risks associated with the remaining concentrated position. Even without requiring leverage to fund new investment, the existing nonconcentrated portion of an investor's portfolio can be organized into a complementary fund.

Complementary funds are funds designed to maximally diversify security-specific risk rather than overall market risk. They can be built either elsewhere in the portfolio or through borrowed funds from one of the approaches that use leverage.

The "completion fund" is similar but does not go as far in reducing overall portfolio risk; it is designed to replicate the behavior of a market index by investing only in stocks that resemble the parts of the index not represented by the initial holdings. But a complementary fund, as defined here, is a different animal. Unlike a completion fund, it does not assume that the market index is the best available trade-off between risk and return. Also, unlike a completion fund, it is applicable even to cases where the concentrated risk position is too extreme to bring into harmony with an index without some form of leverage and hedging—and all the complications noted earlier.

Pooling

Other approaches involve loss of control of the original concentrated ownership position in exchange for the benefits of a diversified portfolio without triggering a capital gains tax.

Exchange Funds. The best example is an "exchange fund." A number of investors contribute their various concentrated positions to a partnership (typically a private limited partnership) or similar entity, and through this pooling, each investor increases diversification of his or her holdings. To qualify as a nontaxable event, the exchange fund is required to hold a material percentage of illiquid investments. This requirement has often been met through buying real estate by using additional borrowing, for which the stock portfolio is the collateral. The strategy may or may not entail a significant waiting period (a "lockup" period) before the investor can withdraw funds.

The consequent introduction of additional leverage and liquidity risk, albeit in a pooled investment, may increase risk, thereby frustrating the original risk-reduction intent.

Finally, exchange fund investments are specific to the contributions of a limited number of contributors in each fund and may be highly clustered in a few industries—therefore, not ideally diversified.

Charitable Remainder Trusts. If the investor is willing to give up both control and a significant part of the value of the concentrated stock, he or she may pool it by donating it to a charitable remainder trust, which may sell it tax free to obtain a different portfolio. The investor receives both a specified amount of future income and an immediate tax deduction for the portion that the IRS expects will become a charitable gift. With proper planning, much of this income can be realized from capital gains in the trust (or even from tax-exempt bonds). The remaining principal after death will pass to the benefit of the associated charity.

This approach, and its many variations, makes sense only for amounts of money that are large enough to justify the necessary legal assistance and only if the investor would have been a donor to the charity in any case. Community foundations and other charitable entities that routinely pool donations from many individuals often have packaged programs that can mitigate some of the legal expenses and include professional investment management of the ongoing portfolio.

Summary

The question of how to deal with concentrated positions carrying large unrealized capital gains is often troublesome because it requires both acumen in tax reduction and an objective approach to relinquishing assets to which the investor may be emotionally attached. For moderate risks and amounts, a targeted outright sale may be optimal. Otherwise, three broad practical approaches are possible:

- Borrowing can raise funds for diversification and dealing with the consequent risk management through some combination of short sales, option collars, or prepaid variable forwards; care must be taken that unanticipated tax or fee complications not spoil the long-term benefit.
- In complementary funds, the concentrated position is left in place but other parts of the balance sheet are revised to lower risks for the total portfolio.
- Pooling with other investors or donors can be effected through exchange funds or charitable remainder trusts.

11. Assessment and Benchmarking for Private Wealth

Chapter 7 presented the basics of performance measurement for taxable investors. This chapter represents a starting point for more comprehensive approaches to assessment and benchmarking. Its narrative is from the viewpoint of the informed wealthy investor.

A theme that has run throughout this book is the highly individualized nature of each investor's circumstances; not only do investors differ significantly from each other, but their circumstances are usually subject to significant changes over time. The usual benchmarking techniques based on risk-adjusted gross returns are worse than unsuitable—they can be seriously misleading.

An appropriate assessment method for private wealth must meet, at a minimum, the following criteria:

1. Risk and return measures must ultimately extend to the question of purchasing power.

2. The tax inputs in the calculations must be idiosyncratic to the specific investor; they cannot be general tax rates.

3. The advisor must have a clear, quantified understanding of at least the minimum wealth and spending levels that must be maintained at all times.

4. If the investor is responsible for other family members or charities, the analysis of the investment plan and its performance should take these people or organizations into account—their available assets, spending/saving, and taxation.

Measuring Return as Purchasing Power

Chapter 4 introduced the four critical factors that have an impact on private wealth:
* investment expenses,
* taxes,
* inflation, and
* consumption.

These factors can be quantified as adjustments to the gross return measures typical of investment performance reporting. Measures of gross return are useful for comparing one manager with another as to ability (or luck). Typically, these benchmarks are either a universe of comparable managers or an index related to the style of the manager. Primarily, these kinds of measures assess security selection skills and, to a lesser extent, trading acumen and costs. These measures may have no relevance, however, for assessing the ability of a manager to meet the needs and objectives of a specific client.

For an illustration of the four-factor analysis, consider this simplified case of an investment account of $5 million consisting of 60 percent stocks and 40 percent bonds. The stock performance in the past year was 8 percent a year, consisting of 6 percent price appreciation and 2 percent dividends, and the bond performance (income only) was 4 percent a year. Turnover averaged 50 percent a year (which is low by most active standards), and a third of the price appreciation was short-term capital gains (2 percent of the 6 percent) and the rest was long-term capital gain (4 percent of the 6 percent). Investment management fees were 1 percent. Inflation was 3 percent. The tax rate for long-term capital gains and dividends was 15 percent, and the tax rate for interest and short-term capital gains was 35 percent.

Consider a comparison of this performance for a tax-exempt institutional investor with the same performance for a private, taxable investor. Both had a gross blended return of 6.4 percent and, less the management fees, a net-of-fees return of 5.4 percent.

The institutional investor has a real return (less inflation of 3 percent) of 2.4 percent. The real value of the assets will double in about 30 years.

For the taxable investor, the net-of-fees return is also 5.4 percent, but then taxes begin to change the picture. The tax components are shown in **Table 11.1**.[52] After subtracting inflation (3 percent) from the after-tax return shown in Table 11.1, the result is a net after-tax real return for the individual investor of only about 1 percent, which will take about 70 years to double.

Table 11.1. After-Tax Return Components for the Taxable Investor

Tax Component	Computation	Result
Short-term gain	60% × 6% × 1/3 × (1 − 35%)	0.78%
Long-term gain	60% × 6% × 2/3 × (1 − 15%)	2.04
Dividends	60% × 2% × (1 − 15%)	1.02
Bond yield	40% × 4% × (1 − 35%)	1.04
Total after-tax blended return		4.88%

---

[52]Note that in this example, unrealized gains are treated as if liquidated because, as shown in Part II, the government "owns" this profit's interest. Although the government's holding is contingent, only the timing of the recognition is up to the taxpayer.

If spending out of the account is limited to the real after-tax return generated, the amount of real purchasing power available each year for the individual from this $5 million account will be only about $50,000. Such an outcome is probably not intuitively obvious to most private investors considering an investment firm marketing a track record of 8 percent for its stock fund and 4 percent for its bond fund; such returns would be viewed as providing a $320,000 gross return (at a blended 6.4 percent) on $5 million.

What return the manager is providing, as returns are conventionally reported, has little direct relationship to the numbers that matter for the taxable investor. No one can spend reported performance numbers. An adequate performance report must clearly disclose the details. By showing the impact of each element that affects net performance prior to consumption/savings, the manager gives the investor a simple but clear picture of the relevant factors.

As a start, a performance report might be constructed as follows:
1. gross return (net of transaction costs) of client portfolio,
2. return net of management fees,
3. return net of #2 and implied taxes, and
4. return net of #2, #3, and inflation.

What benchmark(s) can be used to measure these four line items? The first item can be benchmarked against an appropriate style index. The second item can be indexed against a passive (default) index fund with low or no fees. The third item can be indexed against standard tax rates or optimal achievable tax rates (e.g., a portfolio-weighted blend of long-term capital gains rates for price appreciation, dividend rates for dividends, and tax-exempt bond rates adjusted for the difference in average yield for top-credit/equivalent-duration taxable and tax-exempt bonds). The fourth item is simply the third item adjusted for inflation.

Measuring Long-Term Viability

The long-term sustainability of the investor's investment program is of critical concern—particularly for investors for whom investments generate important sources of cash for consumption. Because the time horizon is different for each investor, the sustainability of the investment program should be quantified.

One approach is to use the actuarially determined remaining life expectancy (remember that this life expectancy is conditioned upon already having reached age *Y*). A cushion factor may be added that consists of additional years but with an asymptotic maximum life span. Based on the investor's remaining actuarial life expectancy, the investment program can be modeled and stress-tested to estimate how long it can be sustained at various expected returns and tax rates (adjusted for inflation and, importantly, consumption). The investment assets can be modeled as an amortizing asset.

After the four factors have been taken into account, the results can be reported in relation to "years remaining" relative to a benchmark actuarial life expectancy. Any assessment report that does not take into account all four factors will be misleading—and potentially ruinous for the client in the long run.

If the investor anticipates supporting others (e.g., a spouse or children), those life expectancies also need to be accounted for in monitoring the long-term survival of the real investment assets.

For investors for whom substantially all of the investment return is being put toward savings, the focus should probably be on the *ultimate* use of the assets. For example, if some assets are intended for a charitable bequest, that target amount can be quantified and the assessment of whether the investment program is on a path to meet the target objectives is relatively simple. For investors who wish to leave money to their children, the analysis might be as follows:

> An investor has set aside $1 million in savings for investment in trusts for newly born twins. The investor would like to achieve at least $1 million in real (today's) purchasing power for each child when the twins are 35 years old. Meeting this goal will require a 2 percent compounded annual "quadruple-net" (net of the four factors) investment return.

The result of this approach is that the target cumulative rate can become the benchmark for the return performance of the investment program in the trusts. All four factors, including consumption, can be accounted for fairly easily, and the analysis of whether the program is on, above, or below the target compounding rate is straightforward. A compelling way to report this information is in the form of a graph with two lines—one for the cumulative target wealth as a function of time and one for the actual cumulative wealth.

Assessing Risk

Risk affects taxable investors in a number of forms. For example, in the benchmarking process, the advisor must consider risk in the form of interim volatility.[53] The lack of perfectly normal return distributions affects tax-exempt investors as well as taxable investors, but because of asymmetrical tax treatment, taxable investors face the more challenging calculations. Further complicating the advisor's job is that the tax posture of the investor is likely to change over time in ways unrelated to the drivers of return. Therefore, periodic updates are a necessity.

Modeling the value of losses (which can mitigate risk) requires understanding that they may be partly binary. That is, for some investors, large losses will have no offsetting gains and, therefore will have no value. The magnitude of downside risk will be essentially the same for such taxable investors as for tax-exempt investors, although the upside potential will not be.

---

[53] Standard volatility measures should be calculated on the basis of after-tax returns.

Risk assessment can be approached through shortfall constraints—and their alter ego, discretionary wealth. By quantifying the minimum acceptable shortfall threshold for the investor, the manager or advisor can create reporting that shows the amount above or below the crucial minimum, which becomes a different kind of benchmark. This benchmark and its portfolio counterpart need to be adjusted for inflation, because the ultimate goal of all private wealth is purchasing power.

Although subject to well-identified problems, optimizers can also provide useful post hoc information on the portfolio. If the advisor uses gross risk and return inputs based on recent historical performance, the investor's actual portfolio can be compared with an efficient frontier composed of the accessible asset classes on both pre- and after-tax bases (with the use of standard tax table rates). Although far from exact (and subject to important caveats), such a depiction can help the advisor and the client see whether the portfolio is going wide of its intended mark in efficiently balancing risk and return. If the opportunity set of asset classes actually available to the investor has been used, anything showing extreme deviation from the standard tax rate–adjusted efficient frontier should trigger further analysis and inquiry.

The Life Cycle and Changes in the Risk–Return Trade-Off

Even if, hypothetically, the efficient frontier for investment portfolios could be known with some certainty, the investor would still have to decide her or his appropriate risk level and its associated return—that is, the correct location on the efficient frontier. This portfolio choice is driven by more than simply tax adjustments and available investment opportunities, and it is likely to change over time. Endowments may have relatively unchanging risk-and-return locations if they assume functionally infinite investment horizons. Other institutional investors, such as pension funds, may shift their risk–return locations based on changes in how assets and liabilities are matched (overfunding or underfunding). But individual investors are most likely to need a readjustment in their risk–return locations on the efficient frontier as they shift from asset accumulation to asset preservation and, finally, to asset dissipation. In Chapter 2, we introduced the concept of a *life-cycle balance sheet* for use in assessing an investor's discretionary wealth. This analysis can be effectively used to adjust the risk–return trade-offs during an investor's life. For investors who wish to take a less quantitative approach to this issue, we present generally appropriate practices here.

For individuals who have no heirs and no significant charitable goals, the appropriate risk level should decline significantly in old age. The target should be to have enough money to live on through the person' remaining years (using maximum life span, not actuarial life expectancy). For individuals with significant investment assets who have retired and who desire a more modest, perhaps simpler lifestyle, risk taking should also decline. Conceptually, this change can be thought of as a special case of an annuity, although it should be quantified on a worst-case basis so as not to run the risk of a shortfall in funds late in life. In this case, then, the appropriate benchmark will usually move to a lower risk and lower return level.

For investors who are accumulating additional wealth primarily for their heirs, as is common in multigenerational family wealthy management, or those with significant charitable goals, the appropriate strategy may look much like that of an endowment fund with functionally infinite life. That is, the allocation may not change in response to the investor's life cycle.

It is not the amount of wealth itself that dictates the appropriate location of investment assets on the efficient frontier; rather, it is the adequacy of the current assets relative to the future needs and goals of the individual. Because both current and future circumstances are likely to change over time, periodic reevaluation of location is necessary, although for most people, every few years is frequent enough.

The Whole Tax Picture

Affirmative confirmation that the total tax picture is being considered should be a hallmark of first-class private wealth investment practice. The discussion to this point has considered the assessment problem primarily from the perspective of a single investor—and even more narrowly, from the perspective of a single account handled by a manager or advisor. Rarely is life so simple. The two key parts of the next analysis are to identify, taking into account all the combined sources of taxable income, the actual tax posture of the investor and to look at what other persons or entities have assets related to the investor's goals that may properly be taken into consideration in crafting an optimal investment program.

The tax rates used in the previous simple examples are easily found in published tax tables, but rarely do they reflect the real-life complexities of actual investors. Ideally, the investment management process should involve a two-way flow of tax information between the investment manager and the client or the tax advisor. At least once a year, usually at the beginning of the fourth quarter of the calendar tax year, the client's advisor(s) should run a *pro forma* tax return incorporating year-to-date information and estimates for the balance of the year. This process should help establish the actual marginal tax rates for various classes of income and identify opportunities and risks for tax deferral, tax-loss harvesting, and so on. Marginal tax rates can be identified. For purposes of performance reporting, the functional tax rates for various types of income can be used in lieu of the standard tax table rates. Commonly used tax-preparation software is inexpensive and more than adequate for the type of *pro forma* modeling that allows the investment manager or advisor to stay on top of the actual tax posture of the investor.

When this modeling is routine, not the exception, it is likely to produce significant changes in asset classes from time to time, as when the investor is wasting deductions and subject to the alternative minimum tax (see Part II) whereas the investment manager is loading up on low-yielding municipal bonds for the taxable client.

Related Entities and Asset Location

Most of the time, the picture for the individual investor is not complete, even if the financial advisor has access to the individual's personal tax information. Wealthy investors often have other investment entities that need to be considered (e.g., trusts, retirement accounts, and businesses and real estate owned by the investor). These entities may not show up in tax information if they did not generate taxable events in a given year(s). A "consolidated balance sheet" approach may be useful in clarifying how related holdings and entities should be considered in a holistic approach, especially as to asset allocation.

Understanding of the entire picture of asset locations is critical before settling on an asset allocation strategy. Moreover, location and allocation cannot be fixed in a one-time exercise. They should be done annually to ensure that the right asset mixes are in the right pockets—particularly, that rebalancing is done with all the entities in mind. A performance report based on the four factors as applied to the consolidated balance sheet is a way to completely assess whether the investor's goals and needs are being met.

Inflation

Inflation is all too easy to overlook. Inflation can be the slow, unseen factor that erodes wealth irreplaceably. Using almost any measure of inflation is better than using none, but the broad standard measures (e.g., U.S. Consumer Price Index, U.S. Gross Income Deflator) are not likely to adequately represent the inflation changes that affect the wealthy. Instead, custom measures made up of the underlying components of the CPI but with more relevant weightings can be crafted to suit individual circumstances—or to suit at least a prototypical wealthy investor. Keep in mind that even though a custom inflation index may be good for a decade or more, its application needs to be at least annual with respect to performance measurement.

Summary

Approaches to assessing the performance measurement and benchmarking needs of wealthy individuals need to be comprehensive and need to recognize the highly individualized nature of each investor's circumstances:

- Investment returns should be reported net of investment expenses, taxes (realized and unrealized), and inflation.
- Taxes should be calculated on the basis of the actual circumstances in the tax year of the report and should take into account ex-portfolio tax factors.

- Measures of risk need to be adjusted for the actual tax circumstances of the investor and should be reported in the context of the specific shortfall constraints.
- To properly assess a portfolio's purchasing power, measures of wealth accumulation have to take into account inflation and consumption.
- Measures of the long-term adequacy of a plan have to take into account not only the investor's life horizon but also the horizons of relevant others.
- For accurately assessing whether the investor's goals are likely to be met by the plan, the advisor must use an integrated approach that considers *all* the entities holding the investor's monies.

Review of Chapter Summaries

Chapter 1. Introduction and Challenge

The professional investor who is used to managing institutional portfolios faces special challenges when serving private investors:

- the need for customization because of differences in investor situations,
- a huge increase in complexity caused by taxation rules and interlinked portfolios, and
- broader fiduciary responsibilities for private clients, who may be poorly informed and who may need more all-inclusive help than institutional clients.

Good practice in working with private clients requires an ethical standard that

- goes beyond choosing suitable securities to encompass specific attention to after-tax returns and absolute versus relative risk and
- proactively avoids misrepresentation by including investor education in the job—for example, by pointing out how difficult it is to project past performance rather than by merely providing an accurate performance record.

These requirements make private investors more expensive to service than institutional clients and encourage the development of cost-effective ways to meet private clients' needs.

Chapter 2. Theory and Practice in Private Investing

Financial theory oversimplifies the problems of private investors. It provides a starting point, but to be useful, it must be adapted carefully and extensively. The main ideas and adaptations are as follows:

- Most ideas and data available to the public are already well priced, which makes picking stocks, timing markets, and picking good managers problematic for most investors. This situation increases the relative importance of risk and tax management. Investors face a trade-off between risk and return, but specifying it for private investors through utility theory, which is idealized and relates to a single period, is often impractical.
- Markowitz mean–variance optimization is the best tool we have for balancing risk and return efficiently, but its correct implementation requires careful study.
- Option valuation theory teaches us that the choice of when to realize a taxable gain or loss is valuable and is enhanced by dispersion in returns and ratios of market value to cost basis.
- Stochastic growth theory helps us understand how to correctly balance return and risk to achieve long-term goals without triggering shortfalls along the way.

Chapter 3. Life-Cycle Investing

Combining stochastic growth theory with the notion of avoiding interim shortfalls leads us to a framework for

- managing discretionary wealth as the key to avoiding shortfalls and achieving long-term financial goals and
- expanding the investor's balance sheet to include implied liabilities, such as capitalized retirement, lifestyle maintenance, and taxes for unrealized capital gains, and to include implied assets, such as capitalized employment-related savings and unvested benefits.

The resulting framework for financial planning, which should be contingent on both age and financial outcomes, guides life-cycle investing, which involves

- summarizing current risk attitudes in the ratio of assets to discretionary wealth,
- subjecting plans to a disciplined review and revision as discretionary wealth and investment environment circumstances change, and
- clarifying the need to address flexibility, end-of-life risk reduction, and plans for excess wealth disposition.

Chapter 4. Lifestyle, Wealth Transfer, and Asset Classes

The key points to check in evaluating the investment needs of the HNW investor are as follows:

- Ascertain the major components of expenditure liability and categorize them from necessity to highly discretionary.
- Ascertain how much in the way of expenditures is required and, of that amount, how much is consumption and how much is non-consumption spending.
- Ascertain the investment horizon, not of the investor alone but also of the others who may rely on or succeed in the ownership of the investment assets (e.g., family members, charities).
- Consider the entire family wealth picture in terms of the (current and long-term) intentions of the investor and the opportunity to locate assets in the most optimal way among family members.
- Consider charitable intentions carefully in terms of the high value for tax deferral.
- Carefully consider the interplay between taxation and inflation as they effect net investment returns relating to maintaining long-term purchasing power.
- Finally, when making allocations among asset classes, take into account fees and costs, taxes, inflation, and consumption—not simply optimization of gross returns.

Chapter 5. Overview of Federal Taxation of Investments

The major points of this chapter can be summarized by considering the key questions related to taxes that the investor or investment advisor should ask when analyzing an investment.

First, what is the *character* of the components of expected return:

- ordinary income;
- dividends;
- long-term capital gain;
- short-term capital gain;
- asset class–specific tax rates—collectibles, real estate, recaptured depreciation, oil and gas depletion allowances, and so on;
- federal tax exemption;
- state/local tax exemption;
- foreign income subject to withholding?

Second, given the character of the income, the AMT, and the limitation on deductions, what will be the effective marginal tax rate for the *n*th dollar of return?

Third, what deductions, expenses, or offsets are available to reduce the tax on the investment return? Does this investment make the most efficient use of those potential benefits? Will the taxpayer be subject to the AMT, and if so, how will being subject to the AMT affect the net treatment of taxable income?

Fourth, especially for periods of fewer than 12 months, what is the anticipated holding period of the investment?

Fifth, how will potential future changes in tax rates affect the after-tax risk and return attractiveness of the investment?

Finally, how will the long-term attractiveness of the investment be affected by the application of the estate tax?

Chapter 6. Techniques for Improving After-Tax Investment Performance

Investment tax strategies fall into a few broad categories:

- Convert the character of taxable return from high-tax ordinary income or short-term capital gains into low-tax long-term capital gains.
- Delay the recognition of gain or income for long periods of time.
- Hold off the recognition of gain or income until death so that only the estate tax, if any, applies.
- Create voluntary losses to offset current gains.
- Use government-sanctioned tax-sheltering vehicles (e.g., retirement accounts or insurance wrappers) to defer or eliminate taxation of investment returns.

Even when these various strategies have superficial appeal, however, the investor should be cautious to analyze the costs involved and should carefully weigh cost against the possible savings. Tax savings that may be only temporary may not be worth the up-front costs.

Although general rules of thumb are a good starting point (for example, municipal bonds are suitable for taxable investors), a complete understanding must include a detailed analysis of the investor's specific tax circumstances—now and *in the future.* This analysis must take into account *income and deductions from all sources* and an estimate of the *final disposition* of the investment assets. Investment advisors should also recognize that the tax rates and rules are constantly changing, so savings that depend on no changes in the status quo of the current tax rules may evaporate unpredictably in the future. Stein (2004a) provides an analysis of the impact of future tax increases.

Chapter 7. Institutional Money Management and the High-Net-Worth Investor

HNW investors, with needs that are both complex and far more heterogeneous than typical institutions, represent a great challenge to the investment professional. In an institutional investment process, the vast majority of intellectual effort is dedicated to forming advantageous expectations about the future return distributions of financial assets. Relatively little effort is expended on adapting the investment process to the needs and preferences of specific investors. Effective investment management for the HNW individual requires that the area of relative emphasis be reversed, giving precedence to the intelligent adaptation of the investment process to the needs of the individual.

Minimization of taxes must be considered a crucial element of performance along with pre-tax return and risk. What matters is not how much return investors make but how much they get to keep.

Absolute returns may be of equal or greater importance than market-relative returns for the HNW investor.

Convincing clients as to what is really in their best interests (and thereby attracting and retaining clients) may not be easy. Therefore, as a business, investment management for HNW investors has particular challenges.

Chapter 8. Portfolio Management as a Manufacturing Process

"Portfolio manufacturing" is a concept dealing with how an investment firm should organize its activities so as to provide high-quality services appropriate to the heterogeneous needs of HNW investors in a cost-effective fashion. Many, although not all, of the differences among HNW investors revolve around taxes. Tax-aware investing considers

- balancing the need to sell appreciated securities for investment reasons (diversification, security selection) against the need to not sell them for tax reasons;
- balancing the need to sell at a loss for tax reasons against the need to not sell them for investment reasons; and
- harmonizing the purchases and sales within tax periods.

Chapter 9. Individual Retirement Plans and Location

Retirement accounts, although nearly universally recommended by investment advisors, are not for everyone—especially very wealthy individuals. Whenever IRPs are considered, attention needs to be given to

- potential changes in future tax rates,
- trade-offs between low current tax rates and higher deferred withdrawal tax rates,
- the potential need for cash before withdrawals can be made without penalties,
- the likelihood of gain recognition even for low-tax-rate investments, and
- the relationship between the retirement account and the estate plan.

In summary, asset allocation and asset location for individual investors involve a holistic consideration of which assets are to be held inside and outside the retirement account in light of the likely tax consequences. The approach involves considering the timing of the person's needs for cash, the benefits of tax deferral, relative tax rates, and issues of rebalancing.

Chapter 10. On Concentrated Risk

The question of how to deal with concentrated positions carrying large unrealized capital gains is often troublesome because it requires both acumen in tax reduction and an objective approach to relinquishing assets to which the investor may be emotionally attached. For moderate risks and amounts, a targeted outright sale may be optimal. Otherwise, three broad practical approaches are possible:

- Borrowing can raise funds for diversification and dealing with the consequent risk management through some combination of short sales, option collars, or prepaid variable forwards; care must be taken that unanticipated tax or fee complications not spoil the long-term benefit.
- In complementary funds, the concentrated position is left in place but other parts of the balance sheet are revised to lower risks for the total portfolio.
- Pooling with other investors or donors can be effected through exchange funds or charitable remainder trusts.

Chapter 11. Assessment and Benchmarking for Private Wealth

Approaches to assessing the performance measurement and benchmarking needs of wealthy individuals need to be comprehensive and need to recognize the highly individualized nature of each investor's circumstances:

- Investment returns should be reported net of investment expenses, taxes (realized and unrealized), and inflation.
- Taxes should be calculated on the basis of the actual circumstances in the tax year of the report and should take into account ex-portfolio tax factors.
- Measures of risk need to be adjusted for the actual tax circumstances of the investor and should be reported in the context of the specific shortfall constraints.
- To properly assess a portfolio's purchasing power, measures of wealth accumulation have to take into account inflation and consumption.
- Measures of the long-term adequacy of a plan have to take into account not only the investor's life horizon but also the horizons of relevant others.
- For accurately assessing whether the investor's goals are likely to be met by the plan, the advisor must use an integrated approach that considers *all* the entities holding the investor's monies.

Appendix A. More on Location

What if the assumptions behind the studies cited in Chapter 9 should change? Can investment advisors derive good answers on asset location for themselves? Many readers who are only moderately quantitatively oriented will be able to do so. All one needs is a passing familiarity with matrix operations and an Excel spreadsheet program.[54]

Decisions on what kind of, and how much, investment assets to put in tax-advantaged vehicles can be made in many ways. At one extreme, decisions can be based entirely on rules of thumb. At the other, one might try to build tax implications, portfolio turnover, actuarial life, and return distributions into a large period-by-period simulation to optimize the total portfolio according to various measures of investor preference.

Mean–variance optimization is an intermediate approach. In this appendix, we show how location analysis through mean–variance optimization can be made practical for customized treatment of individual clients. The problem can be approximated as Markowitz mean–variance optimization by converting the tax effect of multiperiod tax payments to a nearly mathematically equivalent single-period rate.

Mean–variance optimization is often criticized as being overly sensitive to input estimation errors, but this weakness is a by-product of putting large amounts of assets into the problem without taking steps to minimize the impact of errors in estimation, which otherwise tend to increase as the square of the number of assets represented in a covariance matrix. To avoid dealing with this issue, in this appendix, we limit ourselves to five assets. The happy by-product is the possibility of illustrating a simple do-it-yourself solution in an Excel spreadsheet.

A strong advantage of our self-help approach is that it can be easily adjusted to specific circumstances, such as changed tax rates. It also allows one to jointly optimize asset location across taxable and tax-advantaged buckets, thereby optimizing the overall proportion of equities to bonds. The more typical approach of first deciding on the overall asset *allocation* (e.g., between stocks and bonds) and then deciding where to put them with respect to *location* is suboptimal.

To fit the location problem to the needs of the specific private investor, we precede conventional asset allocation with two additional steps. The first is that, rather than have the advisor ask the investor for a subjective risk preference, we use

---

[54]A working copy of the example used here may be available for download at www.wilcoxinvest.com or by e-mailing jwilcox@wilcoxinvest.com.

the discretionary wealth approach described at the end of Chapter 2 and have the advisor ask for estimates of implied assets and liabilities. The *risk-aversion coefficient* for the mean–variance optimization will be half the ratio of assets to the resulting net discretionary wealth. Second, we transform the multiperiod taxes that would have to be paid into an effectively equivalent, "as if," tax rate for a single period.

For this second process, we need to translate the taxes paid on liquidation at posted rates to the equivalent effective single-period tax. To do so, we estimate the tax that, if paid annually, would produce the same final result.[55]

We can estimate an effective tax rate, T^*, such that

$$[1 + r(1 - T^*)]^n = (1 + r)^n (1 - T) + T, \qquad (A1)$$

where:

 r = expected compound price return of the asset class

 T = final posted tax rate

 n = number of years until liquidation

When dividends are included, we can use a weighted tax rate, T^{**}, which is derived from T^*, and the dividend tax rate, T_D. To calculate T^{**}, note that

$$(1 - T^{**})\text{Total return} = (1 - T_D)\text{Dividend yield} + (1 - T^*)\text{Price return}. \qquad (A2)$$

As an example of how effective tax rates vary from the nominal rates, note from Equation A1 that if the expected compound growth rate of a bond portfolio in an individual retirement account (IRA) with interest reinvested is 6 percent but a 35 percent tax will be paid at its liquidation in 15 years, effective tax rate T^* is 26.7 percent. If the expected compound *total return* (because dividends are not taxed in the IRA) of a stock portfolio in an IRA is 10 percent in the same circumstances, the effective tax rate will be approximately 22.5 percent.

We have simplified the estimation of the effective tax rate by taking out all the uncertainties. With the spreadsheet to be described, however, checking the sensitivity of final answers to variations in estimated effective tax rates is easy.

The example in **Exhibit A1** illustrates holding hypothetical stocks and taxable bonds inside and outside an individual retirement account.[56] Given the hypothetical inputs in the shaded boxes in Exhibit A1, the ideal solution in terms of location weights is shown in the "Ideal weights" row below actual or input weights. How is this solution determined?

---

[55] Exactly the same consideration applies to capital gains taxes in fully taxed locations because the effective tax rate may be reduced through compounding long-term holdings; it may even be reduced to zero through a charitable contribution or a tax-exempt estate.

[56] The example uses Microsoft Excel with the "Solver" add-in. It also incorporates a macro overlay that allows the optimization to be run by a single click, but that overlay is an unnecessary refinement.

Exhibit A1. Location Problem Inputs and Ideal Solution

		To find best location of assets in low-tax buckets: Change inputs in colored [shaded] boxes as desired.		
PROBLEM INPUTS				
Financial assets	$462,000			
Implied assets	200,000	Press to optimize weights (except for fixed residual)		
Financial liabilities	240,000			
Implied liabilities	$300,000			

	High-Tax Stocks	Low-Tax Stocks	High-Tax Bonds	Low-Tax Bonds	Residual Assets
Actual weights	10.0%	5.0%	15.0%	10.0%	60.0%
Ideal weights	21.3	0.0	0.0	18.7	60.0
Difference	11.3%	−5.0%	−15.0%	8.7%	0.0%
Mean pretax return	12.0%	12.0%	6.0%	6.0%	8.0%
Std. dev. pretax return	20.0%	20.0%	6.0%	6.0%	12.0%
Tax rate	15.00%	22.00%	35.00%	15.00%	20.00%
Return correlations					
High-tax stocks	1.00	1.00	−0.10	−0.10	0.50
Low-tax stocks	1.00	1.00	−0.10	−0.10	0.50
High-tax bonds	−0.10	−0.10	1.00	1.00	0.40
Low-tax bonds	−0.10	−0.10	1.00	1.00	0.40
Residual	0.50	0.50	0.40	0.40	1.00
Maximum weight	100.00%	20.00%	100.00%	20.00%	60.00%
Minimum weight	0.00	0.00%	0.00%	0.00%	60.00%
Maximum low-tax weight	20.00%				

The example incorporates five asset classes for a mean–variance optimization: stocks in and out of tax-advantaged plans, bonds in and out of tax-advantaged plans, and the remainder of the portfolio. An aggregate balance sheet is used to calculate discretionary wealth and consequently to provide a default aversion to risk. The tax rates are purely hypothetical, illustrative "effective tax rates."[57] An additional constraint is included to prevent the sum of the "low-tax" categories from exceeding the tax-advantaged plan capacity. Residual assets are, in this example, constrained to their initial values.

---

[57]The 22 percent tax rate for "low-tax" stocks is not an error; it is intended to illustrate the possibility that the effective tax rate on an IRA can be quite high because it is based on ordinary income tax rates. In this example, it makes the answer for ideal weights easy to guess.

The ideal weights are estimated by maximizing the risk-adjusted after-tax portfolio return: the expected portfolio after-tax return less the product of risk aversion and portfolio after-tax return variance. The intermediate calculations are worked out in **Exhibit A2**. To follow the logic, the reader needs to know what is meant by "matrix multiplication" and "matrix transposition." Textbooks and online sites are sources of explanations, and these functions are implemented as built-in operators in Excel.

Exhibit A2. Location Problem: Interim Calculations

Discretionary wealth fraction		18.43%		Low-tax total weight	19.00%
Appropriate risk aversion		2.71		Leverage	5.43
				Total weights	100.00%
After-tax rate	85.0%	78.0%	65.0%	85.0%	80.0%
After-tax mean	10.20	9.36	3.90	5.10	6.40
Mean contributions	2.1683%	0.0%	0.0%	0.9559%	3.8400%
After-tax risk	0.17	0.156	0.039	0.051	0.096
After-tax risk matrix	0.17	0.0	0.0	0.0	0.0
	0.0	0.156	0.0	0.0	0.0
	0.0	0.0	0.039	0.0	0.0
	0.0	0.0	0.0	0.051	0.0
	0.0	0.0	0.0	0.0	0.096
Covariance matrix	0.0289	0.0265	−0.0007	−0.0009	0.0082
	0.0265	0.0243	−0.0006	−0.0008	0.0075
	−0.0007	−0.0006	0.0015	0.0020	0.0015
	−0.0009	−0.0008	0.0020	0.0026	0.0020
	0.0082	0.0075	0.0015	0.0020	0.0092

The contributions to portfolio mean return are the weighted after-tax mean returns (i.e., the products of the after-tax means and the weights for each asset).

Calculation of the after-tax covariance matrix begins with putting the after-tax standard deviations of return into a diagonal after-tax risk matrix. This square matrix has the standard deviations of return on the diagonal and zeros elsewhere. Matrix-multiply this diagonal after-tax risk matrix, the correlation matrix, and this diagonal after-tax risk matrix again to calculate the covariance matrix.

The weights, means, and covariance matrix, together with a default risk-aversion trade-off, are the ingredients of mean–variance optimization. Following the discretionary wealth approach, one uses half the leverage (the ratio of assets to discretionary wealth) as the risk-aversion parameter.

Finally, the optimized result and some interesting portfolio statistics are calculated in **Exhibit A3**.

Exhibit A3.	**Location Problem: Results**		
Portfolio mean return	0.0696	**Mean return**	6.96%
Portfolio variance	0.0072	**Portfolio risk**	8.47%
Markowitz objective	0.0502		
Expected growth rate of discretionary wealth			27.24%

The portfolio mean return is the sum of its individual contributions. The portfolio variance is more complicated. It is the sum of the entries in a weighted covariance matrix, which is the matrix product of the weight vector, covariance matrix, and transposed weight vector. The Markowitz objective that was maximized is defined as the portfolio's mean return minus the product of the risk aversion and the portfolio variance.

Another concept to become familiar with is the *expected growth rate of discretionary wealth*; it is needed in Appendix B for solving the problem of deciding what to do with concentrated risk positions. The expected growth rate is approximated as the mean return on discretionary wealth minus half the variance of the return on discretionary wealth. Mean return on discretionary wealth is the mean return on assets times the leverage. Variance of the return on discretionary wealth is the portfolio variance times the squared leverage.

The ideal weights for each of the stock and bond asset classes in this example are initialized by using the actual weights; then, they are automatically varied by using Excel's Solver, which is set in motion by activating the button as indicated ("Press . . .") in **Exhibit A1** until the resulting Markowitz objective can no longer be improved. In this case, because leverage is fixed, the maximum Markowitz objective also maximizes the expected growth rate of discretionary wealth.

In the example shown in the exhibits, all stocks are ideally put into the so-called high-tax location and all bonds are put into the low-tax location, just as one would expect, so the result is intuitive.

Appendix B. More on
Concentrated Risk

Often an advisor wants to know in what circumstances selling part or all of a concentrated risk position would be worthwhile even if the investor would have to pay taxes on the results. This choice should be the first option checked before going to the expense of hiring assistance in pursuing the more complex alternatives that avoid outright sales discussed in Chapter 10.

At one extreme in assessing outright sales, the advisor may rely on rules of thumb. At the other, the advisor might undertake period-by-period Monte Carlo simulations and stochastic dynamic programming models to find an answer. Mean–variance optimization offers a middle ground—but one that should be used with some care.

The description of the do-it-yourself spreadsheet solution we offer here depends on some terms defined in more detail in Appendix A, which addressed the simple problem of ongoing location of securities in taxable versus tax-advantaged buckets. We remind the reader that Appendix A and Appendix B require some familiarity with matrix operations, which will aid in following the logic. Access to an Excel spreadsheet incorporating the "Solver" add-in will be helpful in replicating the results.[58]

A Broad Objective Function

When significant changes in the investor's total discretionary wealth are involved, as when a large tax is paid, mean–variance optimization becomes part of a larger perspective that allows for changes in discretionary wealth affecting leverage and, consequently, appropriate risk aversion. It is not enough to simply maximize after-tax $E - LV/2$ (where L is leverage, E is expected single-period return, and V is variance). Such maximization assumes that leverage is constant, as in Markowitz mean–variance optimization. But in this case, because paying a large tax may change leverage materially, the advisor needs to consider the larger issue of maximizing after-tax $LE - L^2V/2$, which is approximately the expected growth rate in discretionary wealth.

In implementing this approach, the advisor can amortize the initial loss in discretionary wealth, because of the acceleration of the tax payment and all the transaction costs, as an adjustment to the expected discretionary wealth growth rate.

---

[58] A working copy of the example used here may be available for download at www.wilcoxinvest.com or by e-mailing jwilcox@wilcoxinvest.com.

The taxes and transaction costs must, like the security returns, be scaled up by leverage to reflect their impact on discretionary wealth.

This larger problem can be imagined in terms of Markowitz efficient frontiers only with difficulty because each change in leverage induces a change in the efficient frontier. That is, the variety of possible effects on discretionary wealth produces not one efficient frontier but a family of efficient frontiers, each with its own best tangent based on a different risk-aversion parameter. Learning to think in terms of effects on expected growth in discretionary wealth over a specified time horizon makes the problem far more tractable than imagining operations on a family of efficient frontiers.

Implementing the Spreadsheet

Exhibit B1 depicts a Microsoft Excel spreadsheet supported by the "Solver" add-in (here, selected by clicking a button). Exhibit B1 focuses on the inputs used to augment the spreadsheet used for location analysis in Exhibit A1. Appendix A describes how the inputs are used to form the expected portfolio return and the covariance matrix. Here, we focus on the new elements in the asset allocation problem.

The advisor needs only four assets—the concentrated stock, any replacement stocks, any replacement bonds (often overlooked as a possibility), and the residual portfolio. The replacement securities should begin with no weight or allocation.

Shaded cells represent the inputs the user can vary. In this case, the portfolio is assumed to be 50 percent invested in the concentrated position. The suggested new ideal allocation is shown (after the button "Press . . ." is clicked) in the row labeled "Ideal weights." In this case, the majority of the concentrated position is to be sold and, because the initial leverage on discretionary wealth is rather high, some of the proceeds are used to buy bonds. How was this solution determined?

Exhibit B1. Concentration Problem: Inputs and Solution

BASIC PROBLEM INPUTS			Expanded Problem Inputs	
			Tax liability discount	
Concentrated stock	$1,000,000		rate	6.00%
			Concentrated stock	
Residual assets	$1,000,000		cost basis	$125,000
		Press to find best	Unrealized gain %	87.50%
Present value of tax liability	$ 103,962	current plan for concentrated stock	Current gains tax	15.00
Other liabilities	1,500,000		Future gains tax	15.00%
Initial discretionary wealth	$ 396,038		Years to liquidation	4
Initial discretionary wealth %	19.80%		Future tax liability	$131,250

	Concentrated Stock	Replacement Stocks	Replacement Bonds	Residual Assets
Initial weights	50.0%	0.0%	0.0%	50.0%
Ideal weights	1.4	43.5	5.1	50.0
Difference	−48.6	43.5	5.1	0.0
Trading cost	0.80%	0.20%	0.10%	0.25%
Mean pretax return	15.0%	10.0%	5.0%	8.0%
Std. dev. pretax return	40.0%	15.0%	6.0%	12.0%
Effective tax rate	14.0%	14.0%	35.0%	25.0%
Return correlations				
Concentrated stock	1.00	0.60	0.00	0.50
Replacement stocks	0.60	1.00	0.00	0.60
Replacement bonds	0.00	0.00	1.00	0.40
Residual assets	0.50	0.60	0.40	1.00
Maximum weight	50.00%	50.00%	50.00%	50.00%
Minimum weight	0.00%	0.00%	0.00%	50.00%

The inputs to the expanded problem are given in the upper right of Exhibit B1. They allow calculation of the net present value of the product of the current unrealized gain and a future tax rate (which could be zero), a capital gains rate, or a higher estate tax. Exhibit B1 also has a place to enter the current capital gains tax, which might be at a different long-term capital gains rate or even at a higher short-term gains rate.

A new row for entering trading costs has been added. Note that, as in Appendix A, the effective tax rates to be compounded before the tax is paid may be lower than the posted rate. Finally, if the investor wants to constrain the result so that not all the position can be sold, that information is entered as the minimum weight for the concentrated stock asset.

Exhibit B2 shows interim calculations. The top half shows calculation of the modifications that must be made to discretionary wealth in light of the acceleration of tax payments and the trading costs consequent to changes in the weights. This information is used both in cost amortization and in determining a new appropriate aversion to risk. The bottom half determines expected mean and variance of return of the portfolio after reallocation, in the same way as in the Exhibit A2.

Exhibit B2. Concentration Problem: Intermediate Calculations

Concentrated stock	$ 27,376	Total weights	100.0%		
Total assets	$1,862,411				
Present value of tax liability	$ 2,650	Discretionary wealth %	19.32%		
Other liabilities	1,500,000	Leverage	5.18		
Discretionary wealth	$ 359,761				
After-tax rate	86.0%	86.0%	65.0%	75.0%	
After-tax mean	12.90	8.60	3.25	6.00	
Mean contributions	0.18%	3.74%	0.17%	3.00%	
After-tax risk	34.40%	12.90%	3.90%	9.00%	
After-tax risk matrix	0.3440	0.0000	0.0000	0.0000	
	0.0000	0.1290	0.0000	0.0000	
	0.0000	0.0000	0.0390	0.0000	
	0.0000	0.0000	0.0000	0.0900	
Covariance matrix	0.118336	0.0266256	0.0	0.015480	
	0.0266256	0.016641	0.0	0.006966	
	0.0	0.0	0.001521	0.001404	
	0.01548	0.006966	0.001404	0.008100	

Exhibit B3 shows the criterion to be maximized—namely, the total expected growth rate of discretionary wealth over the time horizon. It comes from, first, calculating the expected rate of growth of the discretionary wealth remaining after payment of taxes and transaction costs and, then, adjusting that growth rate for the known initial loss of discretionary wealth amortized over the time horizon. The adjustment is calculated as the natural log of the fraction of discretionary wealth remaining divided by the time horizon. The total asset portfolio's mean return and risk (as standard deviation) are also displayed.

Exhibit B3. Concentration Problem: Results

Portfolio mean return	0.0709	Portfolio mean return	7.09%
Portfolio variance	0.0088	Portfolio risk	9.40%
Discretionary wealth mean	0.3668		
Discretionary wealth variance	0.2368		
Expected subsequent growth rate of discretionary wealth			24.84%
Current % loss of discretionary wealth			9.16%
Growth adjustment for initial loss			–2.40%
Expected growth rate of discretionary wealth			22.44%

Still More Complicated Situations

How would one use a spreadsheet that augments Markowitz mean–variance optimization in complicated situations? Here are two suggestions designed to produce pragmatic, effective results.

Question: What do I do if the concentrated wealth position is composed of several tax lots with different ratios of cost basis to current value?

> *Answer*: To avoid mathematical complications, focus on the tax lot with the highest cost basis first and group the other tax lots with the residual assets; then, recalculate the first tax lot's mean, variance, and correlations. If that tax lot should be sold in its entirety, repeat the process with the next tax lots in descending order of cost basis.

Question: What do I do if future tax rates are uncertain, as is the case with the future U.S. estate tax?

> *Answer*: Solve separately for several different scenarios and use your subjective probability of each scenario to construct a weighted-average allocation.

References

Ait-Sahalia, Yasine, Jonathan A. Parker, and Motohiro Yogo. 2004. "Luxury Goods and the Equity Premium." *Journal of Finance*, vol. 59, no. 6 (December):2959–3004.

Apelfeld, Roberto, Gordon B. Fowler, Jr., and James P. Gordon, Jr. 1996. "Tax-Aware Equity Investing." *Journal of Portfolio Management*, vol. 22, no. 2 (Winter):18–28.

Apelfeld, Roberto, Michael Granito, and Akis Psarris. 1996. "Active Management of Taxable Assets: A Dynamic Analysis of Manager Alpha." *Journal of Financial Engineering*, vol. 5, no. 2 (June):117–146.

Arnott, Robert D., Andrew L. Berkin, and Jia Ye. 2001. "Loss Harvesting: What's It Worth to the Taxable Investor?" *Journal of Wealth Management*, vol. 3, no. 4 (Spring):10–18.

Bernoulli, Daniel. 1738. "Specimen Theorae Novae de Mensura Sortis (Exposition of a New Theory on the Measurement of Risk)." Translated from the Latin by Louise Sommer in *Econometrica*, vol. 22, no. 1 (January 1954):23–36.

Best, Michael J., and Robert R. Grauer. 1991. "On the Sensitivity of Mean–Variance-Efficient Portfolios to Changes in Asset Means: Some Analytical and Computational Results." *Review of Financial Studies*, vol. 4, no. 2:315–342.

Bolster, Paul J., Vahan Janjigian, and Emery A. Trahan. 1995. "Determining Investor Suitability Using the Analytic Hierarchy Process." *Financial Analysts Journal*, vol. 51, no. 4 (July/August):63–75.

Broadie, Mark. 1993. "Computing Efficient Frontiers Using Estimated Parameters." *Annals of Operations Research*, vol. 45, nos. 1–4 (December):21–58.

Brunel, Jean. 2002. *Integrated Wealth Management: The New Direction for Portfolio Managers*. London: Euromoney Books.

Chopra, Vijay K. 1993. "Near-Optimal Portfolios and Sensitivity to Input Variations." *Journal of Investing*, vol. 2, no. 3:51–59.

Chopra, Vijay K., and William T. Ziemba. 1993. "The Effect of Errors in Means, Variances, and Covariances on Optimal Portfolio Choice." *Journal of Portfolio Management*, vol. 19, no. 2 (Winter):6–11.

Chow, George. 1995. "Portfolio Selection Based on Return, Risk, and Relative Performance." *Financial Analysts Journal*, vol. 51, no. 2 (March/April):54–60.

Constantinides, George M. 1983. "Capital Market Equilibrium with Personal Tax." *Econometrica*, vol. 51, no. 3 (May):611–636.

Cremers, Jan-Hein, Mark Kritzman, and Sébastien Page. 2003. "Portfolio Formation with Higher Moments and Plausible Utility." Revere Street Working Paper Series 272-12 (November).

Dammon, Robert M. 1988. "A Security Market and Capital Structure Equilibrium under Uncertainty with Progressive Personal Taxes." *Research in Finance*, vol. 7:53–74.

Dammon, Robert M., Chester S. Spatt, and Harold H. Zhang. 2004. "Optimal Asset Location and Allocation with Taxable and Tax-Deferred Investing." *Journal of Finance*, vol. 59, no. 3 (June):999–1038.

Detzler, Miranda Lam, and Hakan Saraoglu. 2002. "A Sensible Mutual Fund Selection Model." *Financial Analysts Journal*, vol. 58, no. 3 (May/June):60–73.

diBartolomeo, Dan. 1999. "A Radical Proposal for the Operation of Multi-Manager Investment Funds." Northfield Working Paper: www.northinfo.com/documents/61.pdf.

Dickson, Joel M., and John B. Shoven. 1993. "Ranking Mutual Funds on an After-Tax Basis." Working Paper 4393, National Bureau of Economic Research.

Dickson, Joel M., John B. Shoven, and Clemens Sialm. 2000. "Tax Externalities of Equity Mutual Funds." *National Tax Journal*, vol. 53, no. 3, part 2 (September): 607–628.

Fama, Eugene F. 1965. "The Behavior of Stock Market Prices." *Journal of Business*, vol. 38, (January):34–105.

Garland, James P. 1997. "The Advantage of Tax-Managed Index Funds." *Journal of Investing*, vol. 6, no. 1 (Spring):13–20.

Gordon, Robert N., and Jan M. Rosen. 2001. *Wall Street Secrets for Tax-Efficient Investing*. Princeton, NJ: Bloomberg Press.

Gulko, Les. 1998. "An After-Tax Equity Benchmark." General Re Working Paper.

Horan, Stephen M. 2005. *Tax-Advantaged Savings Accounts and Tax-Efficient Wealth Accumulation*. Charlottesville, VA: Research Foundation of CFA Institute.

Horvitz, Jeffrey E. 2002. "The Implications of Rebalancing the Investment Portfolio for the Taxable Investor." *Journal of Wealth Management* (Fall):49–53.

Horvitz, Jeffrey E., and Jarrod W. Wilcox. 2003. "Know When to Hold 'Em and When to Fold 'Em: The Value of Effective Taxable Investment Management." *Journal of Wealth Management*, vol. 6, no. 2 (Fall):35–59.

Ibbotson Associates. 2005. "Stocks, Bonds, after Taxes and Inflation 1925–2004." Ibbotson Associates (1 March).

Jeffrey, Robert H., and Robert D. Arnott. 1993. "Is Your Alpha Big Enough to Cover Its Taxes?" *Journal of Portfolio Management*, vol. 19, no. 3 (Spring):15–25.

Ledoit, Olivier. 1999. "Improved Estimation of the Covariance Matrix of Stock Returns with an Application to Portfolio Selection." Working Paper 3-99, UCLA Anderson School of Management.

Leibowitz, Martin L. 1992. "Asset Allocation under Shortfall Constraints." *Investing: The Collected Works of Martin L. Leibowitz*. Edited by Frank Fabozzi. Chicago, IL: Probus Publishing.

Levy, Haim, and Harry M. Markowitz. 1979. "Approximating Expected Utility by a Function of Mean and Variance." *American Economic Review*, vol. 69, no. 3: 308–317.

Markowitz, Harry M. 1959. *Portfolio Selection: Efficient Diversification of Investments*. New Haven, CT: Yale University Press.

Markowitz, Harry M., and Erik L. van Dijk. 2003. "Single-Period Mean–Variance Analysis in a Changing World." *Financial Analysts Journal*, vol. 59, no. 2 (March/April):30–44.

Mehra, Yash P. 2001. "The Wealth Effect in Empirical Life-Cycle Aggregate Consumption Equations." Federal Reserve Bank of Richmond, *Economic Quarterly*, vol. 87, no. 2 (Spring):45–68.

Messmore, Tom. 1995. "Variance Drain." *Journal of Portfolio Management*, vol. 21, no. 4 (Summer):104–110.

Michaud, Richard O. 2001. *Efficient Asset Management: A Practical Guide to Stock Portfolio Optimization and Asset Allocation*. Reprint. New York: Oxford University Press.

Montalto, Catherine P. 2001. "Households with High Levels of Net Assets." Report to the Consumer Federation of America and Providian Financial Corp.

Peterson, James D., Paul A. Pietranico, Mark W. Riepe, and Fran Xu. 2002. "Explaining After-Tax Mutual Fund Performance." *Financial Analysts Journal*, vol. 58, no. 1 (January/February):75–86.

Quadrini, Vincenzo, and Jose-Victor Rios-Rull. 1997. "Understanding the U.S. Distribution of Wealth." *Quarterly Review*, Federal Reserve Bank of Minneapolis, vol. 21, no. 2 (Spring):22–36.

Rubinstein, Mark. 1976. "The Strong Case for the Generalized Logarithmic Utility Model as the Premier Model of Financial Markets." *Journal of Finance*, vol. 31, no. 2 (May):551–571.

SEC. 2001. "Final Rule: Disclosure of Mutual Fund After-Tax Returns." U.S. Securities and Exchange Commission. 17 CFR Parts 230, 239, 270, and 274 (April).

Sharpe, William F. 1964. "Capital Asset Prices: A Theory of Market Equilibrium under Conditions of Risk." *Journal of Finance*, vol. 19, no. 3 (September):425–442.

Sialm, Clemens, and John B. Shoven. 2004. "Asset Location in Tax-Deferred and Conventional Savings Accounts." *Journal of Public Economics*, vol. 88, nos. 1–2 (January):23–38.

Stein, David M. 1998. "Measuring and Evaluating Portfolio Performance after Taxes." *Journal of Portfolio Management*, vol. 24, no. 2 (Winter):117–124.

———. 2004a. "Do You Anticipate an Increase in Tax-Rates? Deferring Capital Gains Is Not Always the Best Strategy." Commentary, Parametric Portfolio Associates (July).

———. 2004b. "Simulating Loss Harvesting Opportunities over Time." Research brief, Parametric Portfolio Associates.

Stein, David M., Andrew F. Siegel, Premkumar Narasimhan, and Charles E. Appeadu. 2000. "Diversification in the Presence of Taxes." *Journal of Portfolio Management*, vol. 27, no. 1 (Fall):61–71.

Subrahmanyam, Avanidhar. 1998. "Transaction Taxes and Financial Market Equilibrium." *Journal of Business*, vol. 71, no. 1 (January):81–118.

Veblen, Thorstein. 1994. *The Theory of the Leisure Class.* Reprint, first published 1899. Mineola, NY: Dover Publications.

Wang, Ming Yee. 1999. "Multiple-Benchmark and Multiple-Portfolio Optimization." *Financial Analysts Journal*, vol. 55, no. 1 (January/February):63–72.

Wilcox, Jarrod W. 2003. "Harry Markowitz and the Discretionary Wealth Hypothesis." *Journal of Portfolio Management*, vol. 29, no. 3 (Spring):58–65.

Wolfson, Neil. 2000. "Tax-Managed Mutual Funds and the Taxable Investor." KPMG Working Paper.